STEPHEN JEFFREYS
THE CLINK

A Paines Plough Programme/Text published by

NICK HERN BOOKS

A division of Walker Books Limited

A Nick Hern Book

The Clink first published in 1990 as an original paperback by
Nick Hern Books, a division of Walker Books Limited,
87 Vauxhall Walk, London SE11 5HJ

Front cover illustration artwork by Carol Carter reproduced
with permission.

Production costume designs copyright © by Sally Jacobs
reproduced with permission.

Set in ITC New Baskerville and printed in Great Britain by
Expression Printers Ltd, London N7 9DP

British Library Cataloguing in Publication Data
    Jeffreys, Stephen 1950-
    The Clink
    I. Title
    822.914

ISBN 1 85459 073 1

THE CLINK

STEPHEN JEFFREYS

Stephen Jeffreys was born in London. After working variously
as a paint deliverer, teacher, art college lecturer and in the
Jeffreys family business (making billiard tables), he became a
full-time playwright in 1978 after the success of *Like Dolls or
Angels*. This study of a stuntman on the skids was followed by a
two-year residency at the Brewery Arts Centre, Kendal, where
he helped set up the touring company Pocket Theatre
Cumbria, who premiered several of his plays including *Watches
of the Night* (1981), *Futures* (1984) and an adaptation of
Dickens' *Hard Times* which has been given many productions in
Britain and abroad. His Spanish Civil War play, *Carmen 1936*,
won an Edinburgh Festival Fringe First for Communicado in
1984 and enjoyed a successful run at the Tricycle Theatre,
London. He followed this with *Returning Fire* (Paines Plough),
and *The Garden of Eden*, a play for a cast of 150 about
nationalised beer in Carlisle

Valued Friends, a property comedy, played to capacity
audiences during its two runs at Hampstead Theatre in 1989
and 1990, and won Jeffreys the 1989 Evening Standard and
Critics' Circle Most Promising Playwright Award. He has been
involved for many years with the National Student Drama
Festival and was Arts Council Writer-in-Residence with Paines
Plough (1987-9).

PAINES PLOUGH

NEW THEATRE NEW WRITING

'First class company, first class work' *Financial Times*

Paines Plough is Britain's leading touring company specialising in new theatre by new writers. Over the last fifteen years, the company has established an enviable reputation for its high standards of production and performance. The company tours productions all over the country – and now internationally – reaching the widest possible audience. **Paines Plough** passionately devotes itself to seeking the fresh, the vigorous and the immediate. It is committed to writing as part of a total theatre: musicians and dancers, as well as actors, designer and director work together with the writer towards the most consciously theatrical results.

In addition to mounting the best new plays, the company is unique in that it works nationally with writers at all stages of development. We receive and respond to hundreds of scripts each year. We commission plays and provide Workshops for writers as well as Laboratories and public Rehearsed Readings. Recognising that the development of tomorrow's writers and artists relies on practice, experience and adventurous ideas, **Paines Plough** runs an ambitious programme of Courses, Workshops and Events which are often run in conjunction with the company's touring programme. Demand for this aspect of the company's work is growing all the time. **Paines Plough** enters the 1990s ready for further challenges, thinking ahead towards a new theatre in a new Europe.

'The most exciting theatre I've seen for ages' *The Guardian*

The British Council

Arts Council Funded

"Clink"
Lucius

Sally Jacobs
July 90

PAINES PLOUGH and PLYMOUTH THEATRE ROYAL present

THE CLINK

by Stephen Jeffreys

THOMAS BODKIN, a fool DAVENPORT, a Catholic Nobleman GRIDLING, a roarer	**Tony Bluto**
ELIZABETH, a monarch	**Shelagh Fraser**
WARBURTON, a privy councillor	**David Gant**
PERCUSSIONIST, OLD WOMAN	**Didi Hopkins**
BEATRICE, a lady-in-waiting	**Liz Kettle**
LUCIUS BODKIN, a fool	**Mark Lockyer**
JOHN FROBISHER, chief privy councillor HIERONYMOUS BODKIN, a fool, but deceased THE CAPTAIN, a connoisseur of the duel	**Ric Morgan**
THE GUARD JOHN BUTLER, a sorcerer and alchemist THE BISHOP, a prelate DRYSDALE, a pedant	**Keith Osborn**
ZANDA, maidservant to Beatrice	**Taiwo Payne**

Other parts played by members of the Company and by
members of the local community on tour and in London.

There will be one interval

Directed by	**Anna Furse**
Designed by	**Sally Jacobs**
Music by	**Stephen Warbeck**
Lighting by	**Nigel H Morgan**
Assistant Director	**Sarah Le Brocq**
Production and Company Manager	**Paul Crewes**
Deputy Stage Manager	**Sarah Cox**
Assistant Stage Manager	**Christopher Savage**
Wardrobe Supervisor	**Juliet Hardiker**
Graphic Designer	**Carol Carter**

Sets, costumes and props made by Plymouth Theatre Royal Workshops

First performance: Plymouth Theatre Royal 20 September 1990

The Clink was commissioned from Stephen Jeffreys by Paines Plough
Stephen Jeffreys was Paines Plough's Writer-in-Residence, 1987-89

BIOGRAPHIES

TONY BLUTO is an actor and comedian. His theatre and cabaret work include: *Rose English Walks on Water* (Hackney Empire), *Timon of Athens* and *Cowboys* (Red Shift Theatre Company), *The Dead* (Heaven) and *The Victorians, The Dumbwaiter, Zoo Story* and *Strictly Confidential* for Bravura. In 1987 he compered and worked as a stand up comic for the Almeida Theatre/London International Festival of Theatre. Tony has also worked as a stand up comic at the Camden Palace and Paramount City in London and at venues throughout the North of England. His film and television credits include *Jeeves and Wooster, Nightreed, Stormy Monday, Cello, Boon, Casualty, The Paradise Club* and *Blood Rights*.

SHELAGH FRASER – after a scholarship to drama school, she went almost immediately into the West End, and has appeared in numerous productions since, including *The Country Wife* with Joan Plowright, *The Fire Raisers*, David Hare's *Knuckle*, Gallacher's *Schellenbrack*, the Marowitz production of Trevor Griffith's *Sam, Sam*, Mrs Gynt in James Kirkup's adaptation of *Peer Gynt* with Freddie Jones. Other leading roles in *Pygmalion, The Delicate Balance, Who's Afraid of Virginia Woolf, The Slight Ache, The Glass Menagerie, Bedroom Farce* and *Our Own People*. Films include *Raising a Riot, The Staircase, Star Wars, Hope and Glory* and latterly the Oscar winning *Work Experience*. Shelagh has starred in many TV plays by authors including David Rudkin, William Trevor, Peter Terson, John Hopkins and Peter Nichols. She was in Angus Wilson's *Old Men at the Zoo, Frankie & Johnnie* by Paula Milne and was Jean Ashton in *Family at War*.

DAVID GANT – theatre includes: première of David Edgar's *Mary Barnes* (Birmingham Rep and Royal Court). *Harvest, The American Clock* and Stewart Parker's *Nightshade. Fears and Miseries of the Third Reich* (Open Space), *Duet for One*, Prospero in *The Tempest* (Coventry Belgrade) and Anthony Ryle in G F Newman's *An Honourable Trade* (Royal Court, world premiere). He created the role of Prince Michael Baukunin in Mike Stott's *Dead Men* (Traverse Theatre and Perth Festival, Australia). Abel Barbone in Peter Juke's *Abel Barebone*, and the devil in *Playing with Fire* by John Clifford (both world premieres at the Traverse). Peter Biddle's *The True Story of the Titanic* (Sheffield Crucible, world premiere), *Passion Play* (Liverpool Playhouse) and *The Ragged Trousered Philanthropist* (Stratford East London). For Leicester Haymarket: *Oh What A Lovely War*, Mathias in *The Bells* and a tour of *Hamlet*, Ghost and Player King (Old Vic, Europe, Australia, Japan and Taiwan).

Television includes: *The Chelsea Murders, Saphire and Steel, The Gentle Touch, Bloomfield, Pattern of Roses, Moonfleet, A Concert for Mary Rose, Inspector Morse* and Zatopec in *My Family and Other Animals*.

Films include Daniels in *Ghandi*, Mr Seymour in *The Draughtsman's Contract*, Mr Civilette in *Victor/Victoria*, Alphonse Fouquet in *The Scarlet Pimpernel*, *Harem, Firefox* and *The Bearskin*.

DIDI HOPKINS has worked as writer, actress and director in the UK and Europe for the past twelve years. She was co-founder of Beryl & the Perils and has worked with the People Show, Hesitate and Demonstrate, the science fiction theatre of Liverpool, The Albany Combination and Clean Break. TV includes *Unfair Exchanges, Museum of Madness, Comrades* and much TV and radio voice-over work. She spent time out from theatre producing and directing commercial videos and became programme controller for LTV, London Transport's equivalent to the Paris Metro's Television Network. Recently she has been based in Europe with Carlo Boso's international troupes, Tag Teatro, Venice and Lyon Theatre, France. She returned to the UK to direct Molière's *Le Medecin Volant* for the 1990 Liverpool Festival of Comedy.

LIZ KETTLE worked with the 1982 Theatre Co, appearing in *Mistero Buffo, Macbeth* and *Antony & Cleopatra*. Recent theatre work includes *A Girl Skipping* (Graeme Miller) which will tour internationally in 1991, *Bad Air* with sculptor Jim Whiting in Hamburg, *War Dance* (Lumiere and Son), *The Last Days of Nosferatu* (Shadow Syndicate), *La Folie* (Scarlet Harlets).
   Television credits include *Jeeves and Wooster, Capital City, Inspector Morse, Ruth Rendell Mysteries* and *Arm in Arm Together* (Channel 4). She plays Bertha Mason in the film *Exquisite Invalids*, to be released later this year.

MARK LOCKYER trained at RADA. His theatre credits include *Talk of the Devil* (Watford Palace), *Jane Eyre, The Alchemist, Peter Pan, Saved* and *Julius Caesar* (Birmingham Rep), *Carmen* (Derby Playhouse), *Outbreak of God in Area 9* (Young Vic), *The Lady or the Tiger* (Orange Tree), *The Ragged Trousered Philanthropists* (Liverpool Playhouse and Stratford East). For the National Theatre work includes *The Changeling, Bartholomew Fair, Fuente Ovejuna*, and *Ghetto*. His film credits include *Out of Order*.

RIC MORGAN started his career in the West End musical *Fings Ain't Wot They Used T'Be*. Other theatre credits include *Sergeant Musgrave's Dance, Hay Fever, Whose Life is it Anyway?, Privates on Parade*, the Maniac in *Accidental Death of an Anarchist*, Joe Keller in *All My Sons* (York). Recently, he was Victor Franz in Arthur Miller's *The Price* (Dukes Playhouse, Lancaster). He is a performer/director with the improvisation comedy group 'Theatre Machine'. His television credits include *Harvey Moon, Rebecca* and *Lytton's Diary*. Film credits include *The Battle of Britain* and *Ursula and Glenys* (ICA/Channel 4).

KEITH OSBORN trained at Central School of Speech and Drama 1980-83. Repertory work includes: *Julius Caesar*, Kit in *French Without Tears* (Derby Playhouse), Malcolm in *Macbeth* (Ipswich), Peter in *Salonika*, and *Relatively Speaking* (Farnham). Most recently Barberini in *The Life of Galileo* (Contact, Manchester). Tours include: Orlando in *As You Like It* (Cherub Theatre Company). Work at the RSC includes: *The Dillen, Othello*, BT in *Real Dreams* and the 1987/88 Regional Tour of *Hamlet* and *The Comedy of Errors*. Also, Not the RSC Festival at the Almeida: Sycamore in *The Unseen Hand*. At the National Theatre: Frankie in *Roots*. Television work includes *Casualty*.

TAIWO PAYNE trained at St Catherine's Drama School in Guildford. Theatre includes: *World Story Time* (Stratford East), *By the Pool* (Edinburgh Festival), *The Funeral* (Tron Theatre), *The Jungle Book* (Cumbernauld Theatre), *Slaughterhouse 5* (Liverpool Everyman). *The Gods are not to Blame* for Talawa Theatre and most recently *Glory!* by Felix Cross, a Temba Theatre/Derby Playhouse co-production. TV and video credits include *Sorry, Smart Moves, The Lift* and *Where's the Catch?* Taiwo was also Lenny Henry's bouncer for one night!

ANNA FURSE trained at the Royal Ballet School, Bristol and London Universities. During the '70s she worked as an assistant with Peter Brook in Paris, participated in Grotowski's 'Paratheatre' experiments and worked as a writer and performer in the emergent 'New Dance' movement. Productions she has directed (touring the UK, Europe, Asia and the USA) include: (as Artistic Director of Bloodgroup): *Barricade of Flowers, Dirt, Cold Wars, Nature, Strokes of Genius, Clam* and *Pax* by Deborah Levy (Women's Theatre Group), *Burns* by Edward Bond (New Midlands Dance), *The Dead* by Anne Caulfield (Old Red Lion), *Job Rockin* by Benjamin Zephaniah (Riverside), *Stand Up!* with Jack Klaff (Edinburgh), *A Private View* by Tasha Fairbanks (Graeae), *La Folie* by Cindy Oswin (Scarlet Harlets), *On the Verge* by Eric Overmyer (Birmingham Rep), *Find Me* by Olwen Wymark (Drama Studio) and *Medea* by Euripides (Central School of Speech & Drama). Her own play *Augustine* (Big Hysteria) was commissioned by Derby Playhouse. Anna was appointed Artistic Director of Paines Plough in January 1990.

SALLY JACOBS designed many of Peter Brook's RSC productions, and has also been involved with his Paris work. She lived in the USA, for fifteen years, designing and directing in New York and Los Angeles. Since returning to London she has designed *Die Fleidermaus* for the Paris Opera, *Turandot* and *Fiedelio* for the ROH, and *Eugene Onegin* for the ENO. She recently directed a new opera by Peter Weigold for the Garden Venture at Donmar, and will shortly be directing another new piece for the next Garden Venture programme.

STEPHEN WARBECK has written scores for over fifty plays for theatre, radio and television and recently completed a piece for clarinet and five musicians and a series of songs. His scores include the music for *Caucasian Chalk Circle* (Thames Television), *The Resistible Rise of Arturo Ui* and *The Good Person of Szechwan* . He was musical director for the National Theatre tour of *The Mother* and Radio 3's broadcast of *Mother Courage*. At the Royal Court he composed scores for Harwant Bain's *Blood*, Sam Shepherd's *A Lie of the Mind*, Daniel Mornin's *Built on Sand*, Howard Brenton's *Bloody Poetry* and *Greenland*. He also wrote the score for Deborah Levy's play *Ophelia and the Great Idea* and Helen Cooper's *Mrs Vershinin*. He is currently working on two plays for BBC Television.

NIGEL H MORGAN – Recent designs include *Laundry and Bourbon* and *Lone Star* for the Downtown Theatre Company, and *Blood Wedding, Too Clever by Half, The Chester Mysteries*, and *Medea* for the Central School of Speech and Drama where Nigel is Lecturer in Lighting and Sound. Current work includes designs for Caryl Churchill's new play about Romania *Mad Forest*, and Greg Crutwell's new play *Waiting for Sir Larry*, directed by Geraldine McEwan.

"Clink"
Beatrice.

Sally Jacobs
July 90

PAINES PLOUGH AND NEW PLAYS

Paines Plough recognises its responsibility to the individual needs of writers and their projects. The company has been developing a Literary Management department which responds in a flexible and imaginative way to a wide range of material:

THE READERS PANEL
A team of theatre professionals work in collaboration with the Literary Manager and Artistic Director to offer written reports on all scripts submitted.

THE LABORATORY
Ideas, treatments, scenarios, as well as scripts, are considered. Some of these are offered a Laboratory Workshop.

WRITERS' PLAYBACK
Rehearsed Readings with professional cast and director. The emphasis is on the process and audience feedback to the writer, rather than the promotion of a finished play. Writers' Playbacks are usually presented in short seasons at London theatres or in a rehearsal room. The Company also presents Rehearsed Readings in the regions.

SPECIAL SEASONS AND EVENTS
Paines Plough will sometimes produce short seasons of Readings or individual events – for instance Eastern European plays in translation, plays linked to a common theme, Writer-in-performance events (eg. Nancy Reilly from The Wooster Group, USA).

SHOWCASE
A small selection of plays which are fully developed but which Paines Plough is unable to produce, are given a high-profile Rehearsed Reading, which producers and directors are encouraged to attend.

PAINES PLOUGH – A SCHOOL FOR THEATRE WRITING
An important development in the company's work in recent years has been our public work with all processes of theatre, with a particular emphasis on writers. Workshops, Forums, Seminars, Courses, Lectures and Debates are programmed alongside our regular task of responding to unsolicited scripts. During tours, we present concentrated programmes of these events focussed on the thematic issues raised by the productions themselves. These take the form of Roadshows and Festivals of New Writing. Paines Plough's acknowledged expertise in these areas has resulted in commissions for several residencies and residential summer schools. We have worked with people of an age range of between 11 and 80 years. Our overall aim is to offer writers, theatre artists and the general public a constant programme which provokes, stimulates and encourages adventures in new theatre writing.

SEPTEMBER – DECEMBER 1990

THE PAINES PLOUGH ROADSHOW

For the second year running, Paines Plough is delighted to present **The Roadshow**, sponsored by **W H Smith**. The Roadshow is a series of Workshops, Rehearsed Readings, Talks and Discussions which take place alongside the national tour of *The Clink*. The Roadshow is led by professional writers, actors, directors and musicians and aims to stimulate new writing at all stages of development. The Roadshow takes place nationally and culminates in a three week New Writing Festival in London. The Festival will feature some of the best work seen by The Roadshow team on tour including an all-day presentation of short comic pieces by young writers from all over the country.

The Paines Plough Roadshow – made possible with sponsorship from the W H Smith Group, is part of the W H Smith Arts Programme which introduces young people to the arts – especially literature, the theatre, music, dance and design.

PAINES PLOUGH – COMING NEXT

Early Spring 1991: **Feasting on Air**. A co-production with Theatre Centre, the long-established theatre company for young people. A highly original, visual and physical production written by Suzy Gilmour. *Feasting on Air* explores teenage sexuality through a startling adaptation of Hans Christian Andersen's *The Little Mermaid*. Tours nationally before coming to the Lyric Hammersmith Studio in March 1991.

Late Spring 1991: **Augustine (Big Hysteria)**. Commissioned by Derby Playhouse, written and directed by Anna Furse. Based on the case history of an hysteric patient of Dr Charcot in Paris at the end of the 19th century. Augustine was a celebrity in her time, starring in Charcot's public lectures at the Salpetrière Hospital. Freud witnessed Charcot's showmanship, which inspired him to use hypnosis in his Vienna practice two years later – psychoanalysis was born.

This production will tour nationally before playing in Moscow and Kiev (USSR). It plays at the Lyric Hammersmith Studio in June 1991 and will tour abroad during the summer of 1991.

Don't miss out! Join Paines Plough's free mailing list for regular information about productions and events. Phone or send your address to Paines Plough, Interchange Studios, 15 Wilkin Street, London NW5 3NG. Telephone 071 284 4483.

PLYMOUTH THEATRE ROYAL

The Theatre Royal is one of this country's leading regional theatres. In its auditoria, the Theatre Royal and the Drum Theatre, it presents more productions and stages more performances than any other regional theatre. It also has a substantial education and community programme which includes five youth theatres in Devon and Cornwall.

It is the leading member of the South West Theatre Consortium, a unique collaborative venture that has brought together six independent and diverse theatre companies in Devon and Cornwall. This enables a much more productive use of resources, creating considerably more theatre performances in the South West than had hitherto been possible.

Links have been forged with Poland's leading musical producing theatre, the Teatr Muzyczny of Gdynia, and in April 1989 the Teatr Muzyczny's famous production of *Fiddler on the Roof* played in Plymouth.

Since opening in May 1982 the Theatre Royal has been the source of a number of productions which transferred to London including *Peter Pan* (1985-86), *Ross* (1986), *Up on the Roof* (1987), *Brigadoon* (1988-89) and *South Pacific* (1988/89). Theatre Royal productions currently playing in London are the highly successful *Buddy*, at the Victoria Palace Theatre, and *Shadowlands*, the acclaimed play about the love between C S Lewis and the American poet Joy Davidman, at the Queen's Theatre, Shaftesbury Avenue.

The Clink is the third Paines Plough/Plymouth Theatre Royal co-production.

Germinal by William Gaminara (1988) >
'. . . I would recommend this to anyone'
The Guardian
'excellently individual acting . . . excellent
production' *The Independent*

The Art of Success by Nick Dear (1989) ∧
'Inspiring play . . . this production is a triumph . . . excellent performances'
'Paines Plough's latest triumph. Brilliant script, superb performances – Pick of the year'
What's On

PAINES PLOUGH
INTERCHANGE STUDIOS
15 WILKIN STREET
LONDON NW5 3NG
Telephone 071 284 4483
Fax 071 284 4506

Artistic Director	ANNA FURSE
General Manager	TOBY WHALE
Literary Manager	ROBIN HOOPER
Development Officer	DEBORAH REES
Production Manager	PAUL CREWES
Assistant Directors	SARAH LE BROCQ
	ROXANA SILBERT
Press and Marketing	TAYLORS (071 580 0442)
Associate Artist	STEPHEN JEFFREYS
Writer in Residence	APRIL DE ANGELIS
Graphic Designer	CAROL CARTER

Ian Duncalf (Consultant, Accounting Centre of Expertise, BP) is working as an advisor to Paines Plough through Business in the Arts, an initiative of ABSA.

Performances of **The Clink** at Riverside Studios, London are sponsored by INGLENOOK NAPA VALLEY WINES

PLYMOUTH THEATRE ROYAL (0752 668282)

Artistic Director	ROGER REDFARN
General Manager	ADRIAN VINKER
Finance Director	STEPHEN MORRIS
Production and Technical Controller	MAX FINBOW
Theatre Manager	HELEN PALMER
Catering Manager	SALLY HAYNES
Marketing Consultant	MICHAEL HIRST
(seconded by ECC Group)	

Production photographs by Sheila Burnett

"Clink"
Heironymous

Sally Jacobs
July 90

THE CLINK

'A king is a thing men have made for their own sakes,
for quietness' sake. Just as in a family one man is appointed to
buy the meat.'

John Selden

The Clink was first staged at Plymouth Theatre Royal on 20 September 1990.

Characters

LUCIUS BODKIN, a fool
THOMAS BODKIN, his brother, a fool
BEATRICE, a lady-in-waiting
ZANDA, her maidservant
JOHN BUTLER, a sorcerer and alchemist
JOHN FROBISHER, chief privy councillor
AN OLD WOMAN
ELIZABETH, a monarch
HIERONYMOUS BODKIN, a fool, but deceased
WARBURTON, a privy councillor
THE BISHOP, a prelate
DAVENPORT, a Catholic nobleman
THE CAPTAIN, a connoisseur of the duel
GRIDLING, a roarer
DRYSDALE, a pedant
A GUARD

Also: ABRAHAM MEN, VISITING DUTCH TRADE DELEGATES, ICE DWELLERS.

PROLOGUE

*London Bridge. Night. A line of skulls impaled along the parapet. A
single violin plays discomforting intervals. WARBURTON, a
minister of the crown appears. From time to time the hands of beggars
reach up to him in supplication. He ignores them.*

WARBURTON. In London where the reigns of Tudor Queen
   And Scotch incursor merge like seas of fret
   And calm, we find our scene: the streets, the stews,
   The penny-lodging horse-piss stables and the
   Iron gates of Bedlam; also the court,
   Stage of the Mighty – those who stand above the
   Mob like unversed stiltsmen, tottering a moment
   Before measuring their stature in the mire.
   All will stalk here. The abject and the proud,
   Distinct in wealth and place find common cause
   In shared delusion: Conspiracy. This sickly
   Phantasie is dream'd by all. Conspiracy,
   Which thrusts the dispossess'd third son onto
   The throne of power and drops the greasy drab
   Upon the pintle of a king. Oh monstrous dream,
   Oh sickly sweet conspiracy, which, like a
   Gilded bounty ship spied on a far
   Horizon does so pheeze the waking minds of
   Men they must pursue her. Then, drawing fast
   Beside, perceive their prize was but a drifting
   Plague ship, deck'd with a Black Flag. So all
   Is lost upon the instant of the triumph:
   He who thought to glide in stately pageant
   Stands unmoving 'twixt a pike's end and a wall;
   Once carrying all before him in his mind,
   Makes swift dispatch to leave the world behind.

Flourish from the violin. The beggars laugh. The skulls disappear.

Blackout.

Scene One
THE FOOLS

Bare stage. Two men, LUCIUS *and* THOMAS BODKIN, *are performing a routine of acrobatic physical warm-ups. They are an Elizabethan comedy duo. They wear loose, practical clothes rather than 'costumes' and they do not wear clown make-up.* THOMAS, *the elder of the brothers, has the air of an old pro.* LUCIUS *is strange and earnest. They have a large cloth bag with them. After some moments, a* GUARD *comes on.*

GUARD. All right?

THOMAS. Played worse.

GUARD. Double act, eh?

THOMAS. Lucius. Bag there.

GUARD. They're not going for double acts any more. Your single fool, that's the fashion. Saws and riddles. Pithy, a bit deep. Little song at the end. Not your double act. Your solo fool.

   LUCIUS *has opened the bag. It spreads out to become a performance cloth with jesters' equipment arranged on it.* THOMAS *gives orders.* LUCIUS *obeys.*

THOMAS. Masks there. Bladder there.

GUARD. She's seen twelve acts today already. Mostly crap between you and me. No double acts. Still, the word is she hasn't hired anyone yet.

THOMAS. She?

GUARD. The Lady Beatrice. Beneath her father's dignity, this sort of work. Can see his point.

THOMAS. The tambour. The windpipe.

GUARD. What you call yourselves?

THOMAS. The Bodkin Brothers.

GUARD. The what?

THOMAS. We used to be the Brothers Bodkin. Now it's the Bodkin Brothers. Going for a different sort of audience, see?

GUARD. Bodkin.

THOMAS. Cap. Bells. Dildo.

GUARD. Bodkin. Wasn't there a fool called –

THOMAS. Hieronymous.

GUARD. Hieronymous Bodkin, the very man.

THOMAS. Our father.

GUARD. There's a thing. It must be years. Big black beard.
Did a routine taking the piss out of medieval hunting.

THOMAS. That's the one.

GUARD. Saw him, some terrible dive in Southwark. Bloody
great live hawk on his head. Big bugger. And a stuffed hawk
on either hand. A speech and a song and then he'd shuffle
them round. The bird acted dead, you couldn't tell which
one was real. Wrist to head to wrist, shuffled them at
lightning speed, then bit two of the heads off at random.
You could have sworn he'd picked the wrong one, then it
would chirp up and they'd sing a two part catch together.

THOMAS. His last show he did.

GUARD. What?

THOMAS. Pick the wrong one. Blood everywhere.

LUCIUS. Bits of beak.

THOMAS. Bits of beak, yeah, plumage. I still say it was no
accident. The bird had become the star, see.

GUARD. Christ. Hieronymous Bodkin. He was a good fool.

THOMAS. He was a fool's fool.

GUARD. Yeah. Well I'll bring in her ladyship if you're ready.

THOMAS. We're always ready.

The GUARD *makes towards the door, then stops.*

GUARD. Heard the one about the Spaniard with the –

THOMAS. Three foot ruff. Yes we have.

GUARD. I'll fetch her ladyship.

The GUARD *goes.*

THOMAS. Syphilitic ponce.

THOMAS *inspects the performance area gravely, clears his throat,
strikes an attitude or two.*

LUCIUS. Thomas. Let me.

THOMAS. No.

LUCIUS. Just a few minutes of the new stuff. One speech.

THOMAS. There is no new stuff. This is a traditional act. No politics, no arseing around. They know what they're going to get, give it to them. Now, the codpiece gag. When you do your somersault, give it a bit more time, let it register before –

LUCIUS. The codpiece gag! We will not get this job with the codpiece gag, or any of that old material –

THOMAS. If they don't want us, we don't want them –

LUCIUS. There's nothing funny about codpieces any more –

THOMAS. Men have pricks, that is funny, it will always be funny –

LUCIUS. We're talking about a sophisticated audience. Visiting ambassadors and businessmen from the Dutch Republic. It's a new society, a young society, based on trade and success. These people speak five languages and do double entry book-keeping, they don't want to hear songs about bollocks!

BEATRICE *comes in. She's in her late twenties, striking, assertive. She's followed by her maid* ZANDA, *a young black woman who carries a footstool. The* GUARD *stands in the doorway.*

BEATRICE. The Dutch Republic, quite so. Did someone mention the Dutch Republic?

LUCIUS. I –

THOMAS. Thomas Bodkin, ma'am. And my brother Lucius.

BEATRICE. In point of fact there are only two interesting facts about the Dutch Republic: one it is stuffed full of Protestants and two it is stuffed full of money. Politics and commerce. We are wooing the Dutch, gentlemen, and, as with wooing, one moves in orderly stages: the meeting of the eyes, the inclining of heads, the dallying of fingers, then of lips. These have their counterparts in the whisperings of diplomats, the exchange of useless presents and – mark this – in the trade delegation. In the wooing of nations, gentlemen, the trade delegation is like a hand placed upon a thigh. The timing and the pressure must be exact. Do I make myself clear?

THOMAS. Er . . . yes . . . your ladyship.

BEATRICE. My father, being a councillor of state, is occupied
with the weightier side of this event. He has instructed me to
choose the entertainment. The Dutch are a swinish people
much given to strong drink. Their natural churlishness has
stood them in good stead against the Spanish –

She spits copiously on the floor.

They do not take to madrigals and fine wine. They are for
beer and buffoonery. So they must be entertained here, in
the Liberty of the Clink where greater licence is extended,
beyond the City Fathers' reach. I am these Dutch. We are
these Dutch. Entertain us.

The BODKIN BROTHERS *glance at each other, each having
heard something to support their own viewpoint.* THOMAS'*s
authority carries the day and they launch into their traditional act.
He dons the jester's cap and picks up the bladder.* BEATRICE *puts
her feet on the stool for* ZANDA *to cut her toenails.*

THOMAS. By the mass if 'tis not Signor Bordello, newly come,
or so his gait betells, from some house of drabbery. This
fellow is a most notable dealer in flesh, a very fishmonger,
fowl-trader and jack-the-knife i' the shambles. How now,
Signor Bordello, what make you here amongst honest men?

LUCIUS *comes on as Signor Bordello.*

LUCIUS. I cry thee pardon, Master Wart, I took thee for but a
simple fool.

THOMAS. Who takes an honest man for a fool i' the street
makes swift despatch to hell.

LUCIUS. How so, whoreson?

THOMAS. Why, to take an honest man in the street (*Sexual
mime.*) means that man is fallen, and to be deceived that he
is a fool is yourself to be gulled. And if the Almighty will not
let a sparrow fall in the street, sure to let a gull so drop, why
man, 'tis certain brimstone.

They pause for the laugh. ZANDA *who is simultaneously watching
the scene and pedicuring* BEATRICE *looks questioningly at her
mistress.*

LUCIUS. Faith, you equivocate to a hair's breadth.

THOMAS. Indeed sir, I shall prove a most punctilious barber

to your tongue. Let but the smallest mole sprout and Wart shall trim thee. But to't again – what make you here?

LUCIUS. Faith, I am but newly come from business at the Exchange –

THOMAS (*aside*). Indeed I have heard the stews so called, for therein a man may spend freely and yet be called to account when the month is passed –

LUCIUS. Where there is much talk that certain carracks, laden past endurance are become no more than citadels for minnows and the bretheren of the finny drove.

THOMAS. Such a thing can never endure, sirrah.

LUCIUS. Why so, my razoring knave?

THOMAS. A fish, sir, is a slippery thing, and no slippery thing of my acquaintance can be guarded past an hour without –

BEATRICE *has thrown her fan on the floor at the fools' feet. The* BODKIN BROTHERS *stare at it.*

BEATRICE. Zanda, my maidservant, tell these . . . fools . . . if so we may nominate them, how you came to London.

ZANDA *is puzzled, then collects herself.*

ZANDA. My lady, on a pirate ship. I was filched by Spaniards –

BEATRICE *spits copiously on the floor again.*

ZANDA. – from the place you call Morocco. Then, grappled by an English galleon, I was dragged off as booty, manacled and brought for sale in London where my Lord, your father paid –

BEATRICE. So. She does not like to hear about ships.

THOMAS. My lady, I do crave pardon –

BEATRICE. Or carracks. Or galleons. Or fish.

THOMAS. Ah –

BEATRICE. Or war. Or men. Or God, gold and the devil. These things offend her.

THOMAS. My lady, this is too severe.

BEATRICE. Quite so. And she is but one among an audience. Each will have certain . . . calloures which may not be pricked. Every subject is forbidden.

THOMAS. Then . . . then . . . how, my lady, may we please?

BEATRICE. Quite so. You have mistook your art. You are not here to please, but to puncture. I do not wish to be flattered, I wish to be flogged.

The GUARD *swallows hard.* THOMAS *stands on his dignity.*

THOMAS. Then, madam, I must say we are not for you. We are the Bodkin Brothers. I trust you will remember us. Good morn –

LUCIUS. Wait.

LUCIUS *picks up the tambour and a beater. He plays an insistent rhythm, moving jerkily in time to it. After a while, he hands the tambour over to* THOMAS *who, reluctantly at first, keeps the pulse going.* LUCIUS *chants and stamps in time.*

LUCIUS. On the death's head streets where the wind stabs sharp and the ice will never crack
And the beggarmen fight to sell their arse for the froth on a cup of sack
And the watch kick their iron heels in the wounds of the varlet on the rack
And the madmen in power wave their maps in the tower and scream: 'Attack, Attack.'

A voice cries: 'LON-DON LON-DON'
London the dungeon, the sewer
Where fewer have the power
And more are the poor who are huddled at your door
As your teeth set on edge
In the beef that you thieve when you pledge
Your soul to the devil of London
Town and that's what the voice cries out.

LUCIUS *picks up a skull and beats in time with a bone.*

Where the gutters run thick and the gutters run thin with the sewage you can drink from the pumps
Where the bawds are painted ladies and the ladies are pox-ridden frumps
And the coining cozening cardsharp cuts your throat when he turns up trumps
Where the leperman swings on his sticks like a chimp and kicks you with his stumps

A voice cries: 'LON-DON LON-DON'

London the dungeon, the sewer
Where fewer have the power
And more are the poor who are huddled at your door
As your teeth set on edge
In the beef that you thieve when you pledge
Your soul to the devil of London
Town and that's what the voice cries out.

LUCIUS *utters a great cry and smashes the skull open with his forehead. A treacly black liquid oozes out.*

LUCIUS. It's only a trick. Only the fool's trick. This man wasn't really rotten. This pus in the skull. It's nothing to do with . . . PLAGUE!!!

He lunges forward with the skull. Both women flinch. The GUARD *makes to intervene, but* LUCIUS *suddenly smiles. The* GUARD *backs off.*

No offence. There's no offence.

GUARD. Tread warily, son.

LUCIUS. Well. Did I . . . puncture you? Do you consider yourself . . . flogged?

BEATRICE. Is there . . . more of it?

LUCIUS. There could be. I am a very fast boy. A very fast boy indeed. I'm adding to it all the time.

BEATRICE. We will have this fool. On Wednesday next. Report to the kitchens for your bread and broth at six o'clock. You will play after the lutanist. Ten minutes. Could you insert something concerning the manners of our Dutch cousins?

LUCIUS. A pleasure, my lady.

BEATRICE. Then I will send for you. My father will have to school you in the art of diplomacy.

LUCIUS. I shall await your command.

BEATRICE *makes to go.*

And gramercy for the offer of a skillet of gruel. The steam will cleanse my pimples.

BEATRICE *holds the look for a moment, then goes off, followed by the* GUARD.

A pause.

ZANDA *and* THOMAS *both look at* LUCIUS. *Then* ZANDA *goes on her knees to sweep up the toe-nail clippings.*

THOMAS. What was that?

LUCIUS *is wiping the black liquid off with a towel.*

I ask again, what in the bowels of Christ was that? You shad, you pustule. We could have had our thumbs crushed for that.

LUCIUS. It's a dangerous business.

THOMAS. I'm not doing it. Those Dutch bastards'll have our livers on a plate.

LUCIUS. You weren't asked. 'We will have *this* fool.' So said my lady.

He turns to ZANDA *for confirmation.*

ZANDA. He's right. One fool will be enough.

THOMAS. We're finished.

LUCIUS. Good.

THOMAS. I mean it. Don't even think of me as your brother any more.

LUCIUS. I never did.

THOMAS *is packing the gear.*

THOMAS. You're not getting any of the props.

LUCIUS. I don't need props.

THOMAS. It's authentic, all this gear. What you're doing, it's just a fad. The old skills will come back, you see.

LUCIUS. I can't wait.

THOMAS *is packed and ready to go.*

Well, Good Master Wart, you must find some other tweezer to squeeze forth the great yellow stream of your wit.

THOMAS *looks at him then goes.*

LUCIUS *stretches. He lies on the floor, breathing deeply, savouring his triumph.* ZANDA *walks towards him and holds him down, her foot on his chest.*

LUCIUS. And are my lady's feet now neat and trim?

ZANDA. You frightened me.

LUCIUS. No jagged edges which might foul her stockings.

ZANDA. And insulted me.

LUCIUS. I insulted your lady.

ZANDA. Don't cross me, fool. I am not an over-ripe fruit like my lady. I do not relish your puncturing and flogging. I have known real slavery, I do not need the waxen imitation.

LUCIUS *sits up, looks at her.*

LUCIUS. What's your name?

ZANDA. Zanda.

LUCIUS. What I said in my foolery, Zanda. It was for you.

ZANDA. Then I will give you something back. This Dutch business. Don't do it.

LUCIUS. I'm booked, I can't turn it down.

ZANDA. It's not all that it seems.

LUCIUS. I've got no choice.

ZANDA. Take my advice.

LUCIUS *looks at her steadily.*

LUCIUS. You could sell my lady's clippings to a witch.

ZANDA *flicks the clippings in his face.*

ZANDA. You sell them. I have more need of my eternal soul.

ZANDA *goes.* LUCIUS *sits and smiles.*

LUCIUS. Lon-don. Lon-don.

Blackout.

Scene Two
THE MAGICIAN

A spotlight picks out FROBISHER, *a privy councillor.*

FROBISHER. She sits. Hour upon hour. In a pile of favourite

cushions. On the throne.

On the other side of the stage, a light comes up on QUEEN
ELIZABETH, *sitting as* FROBISHER *describes her.*

She doesn't sleep. But she doesn't seem to be awake. Refuses
her bed. Scratches at her bony wrist and demands with her
eyes to be left alone. Sits. Doesn't speak. Even when spoken
to. Foreign policy? Not a flicker. Provisions to be made
against the plague? Won't sign. Important visitors who've
journeyed hundreds of miles for a glimpse of that paper
white face? Will not be seen. Just sits. Sits on the throne.

Immediately, lights come up generally. We are in the shop of JOHN
BUTLER, *a professional sorcerer.*

BUTLER. Well it stops any other bugger getting on it, eh?

FROBISHER. I'm telling you this in confidence, Master Butler.
We wouldn't be worrying if we knew for certain she would
die soon. Supposing she doesn't. Supposing she hangs on for
years.

BUTLER. Does it matter? I thought you boys were in the
coachman's seat these days. Monarchs? Figureheads.

FROBISHER. The next one will be. This one knows the score.
Or used to. Now. Are you going to come up with something?

BUTLER. Oh very droll, Master Frobisher.

FROBISHER. I'm sorry?

BUTLER. Come up with something? What happened to the
rational world, science, the modern society?

FROBISHER. We're desperate. We need something. She hasn't
named a successor. If she pops off in her sleep without giving
the nod to that po-faced Scotchman, we are at the mercy of
every Spanish Don whose uncle knocked off Catherine of
Aragon – and that's two-thirds of the men in Castille by all
accounts.

BUTLER. Mr Frobisher, what am I?

FROBISHER. Christ's wounds, spare me this –

BUTLER. I am a professional alchemist and sorcerer, right? I
am a last link with the irrational past. Three hundred and
sixty-five days a year, I am regarded by you privy councillors
as an old turd decomposing on a tumulus in the middle of

Salisbury plain. Then, once in a blue moon, you get a crisis on your hands, something the world of high finance and backstairs intrigue can't solve, and you come crawling out of the woodwork treating me like the bloody sphinx.

FROBISHER. Just because we come here doesn't mean we believe in you. But we have to be seen to exhaust every possibility. Nothing personal, but I hope this is the last time. One thing I will say for the Scotch pedant, there's no mumbo-jumbo about him. Now come on, don't stand on your dignity and some royal gold will come your way.

BUTLER. I'm a fool to myself.

BUTLER *begins to work, reaching down powders from jars, mixing them in his crucible, scattering salts and creating minor explosions.*

FROBISHER. That's my boy.

BUTLER. There's only a certain amount I can do, she's got Mercury in the worst possible place.

FROBISHER. Do your best for me, John, something to make her talk. Preferably about how fetching her cousin looks in ermine.

BUTLER. Be a funny old world without her.

LUCIUS *comes in.* BUTLER *doesn't stop what he's doing.*

BUTLER. Yes?

LUCIUS. Oh sorry, I'll come back when you're –

BUTLER. What you want?

LUCIUS. Oh, er . . . raising the dead?

BUTLER (*without a blink*). Permanently or just a consultation?

LUCIUS. Oh, just some advice . . . professional advice.

BUTLER. Relative?

LUCIUS. Father.

BUTLER. Dead long?

LUCIUS. Ten years.

BUTLER. Cost you three shillings.

LUCIUS. Christ.

FROBISHER. What am I paying?

BUTLER. You're the crown, I charge what I want.

LUCIUS. Will it work?

BUTLER *stops, looks at* LUCIUS *for the first time.*

BUTLER. What do you do, mate?

LUCIUS. I'm a fool.

BUTLER. Right. If I pay to see you, will you guarantee to make me laugh?

LUCIUS. I . . . well . . .

BUTLER. See what I mean. This geezer here is an advisor. To the Sovereign. But is his advice any good? Get my point? Every man to his mystery. And it *is* a bleeding mystery most of the time.

LUCIUS *puts down money.*

LUCIUS. Three shillings.

BUTLER. Ta. Be with you in a second.

BUTLER *completes his work, hands a potion to* FROBISHER.

Here. To be inhaled. Waft it around, she doesn't need to agree to it, see. Could be drastic. But it'll definitely make her talk. Come back for a repeat in a fortnight if she doesn't say what you want. Two sovereigns.

FROBISHER. You jest.

BUTLER. Come on, John, it all comes out of the common purse. Not as if you'd be improving the highways with it.

FROBISHER *pays.*

FROBISHER. What's in it?

BUTLER. Mystery, John, liquid mystery.

FROBISHER *looks at him, then goes.*

BUTLER. Now then, raising the dead. Ten minutes be long enough.

LUCIUS. Five.

BUTLER *goes to work again.*

Busy this morning?

BUTLER. Always a rush, late January. Goes quiet over Christmas,

then people start remembering their grudges. Liked your
Dad, did you?

LUCIUS. Respected him.

BUTLER. Makes it easier. Now then. Go to his grave. Midnight.
Twelfth chime, chuck the potion roughly where the heart
would be. And stand back with your eyes shielded. And don't
waste time in chit-chat, come straight to the point. The dead
will ramble, it's their biggest fault. Right?

LUCIUS. Thanks.

BUTLER. For a fool . . .

LUCIUS. Yes?

BUTLER. You don't strike me as funny.

LUCIUS. You should see me when I'm working.

LUCIUS *goes.*

Pause.

An OLD WOMAN *comes in. She wears a black dress with a hood
and looks very ill.*

BUTLER. Stay there. No further.

The OLD WOMAN *stops.*

BUTLER. Swellings under your armpits?

The OLD WOMAN *nods.*

BUTLER. And the groin?

The OLD WOMAN *nods.*

Breaking into pus.

The OLD WOMAN *nods.*

By the door. There's some little paper packets of arsenic.
Take two. One under each armpit. Don't bother to pay. Just
take them and go. And if you can find any fruit, eat it.
Remember, under the armpits.

The OLD WOMAN *moves off with the arsenic.*

Or better still, swallow the lot, it's quicker.

She turns. They both make the sign of the cross.

Blackout.

Scene Three
THE EMPRESS

Lights up on QUEEN ELIZABETH, *still sitting on the throne. She looks very old and frail. There are a dozen sumptuous cushions around her. Throughout the scene she stares ahead as if she were really somewhere else. No one succeeds in making eye-contact with her or in attracting her attention in any way.* BEATRICE *is attending on her.*

BEATRICE. Your majesty. Your majesty.

Silence.

I know you're not asleep.

Pause.

Listen. We're all worn out with you sitting there, doing nothing. You'd be less trouble if you were roaming round the Fens on a royal progress. Don't think I don't know what you're up to. This kind of behaviour might impress the scullery maids, but it doesn't cut any ice with me. All this spending days without a word or movement and then coming on distracted. 'A spoon, the spoon my father dropped in the river at Richmond.' So someone brings you a spoon and you hurl it on the floor and go all silent again. Well we've all done that. I had to change my religion three times in a month when I was eight years old, this kind of stuff is second nature to ladies of breeding.

FROBISHER *comes in with the potion.*

FROBISHER. Got the physic. Not cheap, but if it does the business . . .

BEATRICE. What's happening?

FROBISHER. Uncertainty. That's what's happening. Worst thing in the world. The body politic depends upon strong rule. Give the dogs the scent of indecision and they're at your throat. Firm rule is all. Each stair you climb is clogg'd with Catholic schemers, skinny Puritans, and worst, the ragged rousers of the hungry mob who'll serve a turn to any ranting demagogue who'll throw them bread. This long, iron reign could yet be set at naught. The Infanta waits, to gain by stealth what arms could never achieve: a Catholic England tramp'd on by the Spaniard, a servile, lackey land which begs its food from foreigners like an old cat dying in a stranger's yard.

BEATRICE. My father is much of your mind. He asked me to impress on you the importance, in these circumstances, of the visiting Dutch delegation. I've organised the entertainment myself. My father begs that you will appear in person at the feast. As senior privy councillor and greatest in the land after the Queen, your presence will be seen as giving high assent to their nation's link with ours.

FROBISHER. He's right. I will attend this banquet and whatever masques you've chosen. We must steer a Protestant course and calm the city down.

BEATRICE. My father will be pleased.

FROBISHER. Now, Beatrice, you must be witness, as the Queen's chief lady-in-waiting, to a mighty deed.

FROBISHER takes the powder up-stage, places it in a metal censer and sets fire to it.

Plans have been set in motion. Horses have been posted at twenty-five mile intervals along a secret route. Passwords and signals have been agreed. All we want from her is one word and the succession is guaranteed. This inhalation will unlock her mind and tongue and keep the country Protestant and rich.

The powder catches light and burns for a second before settling into a dull glow. Smoke rises up. FROBISHER approaches the QUEEN and wafts it around her.

Christ! It's too strong, I can't . . .

Smoke billows out. FROBISHER can't bear the smell and drops the censer next to the QUEEN. He coughs furiously. ELIZABETH begins to mumble. BEATRICE is on the point of leaving the room. FROBISHER tries to hold his ground.

FROBISHER. She's saying something. What's she saying?

But he is overcome by the fumes. BEATRICE pulls him away to safety. ELIZABETH sits motionless in the mist. She enunciates perfectly.

ELIZABETH. Old though we be and frail of heart and limb
Yet to our God we offer prayer and hymn
In thanks for this boon of surety of mind
As we make haste to leave the world behind.
Thus though no heir have we borne of our own,
Still we name successor to our throne:

Our blessing throw we on that first of names
Our Cousin King, the noble Scottish James.

ELIZABETH *stares ahead. The mist clears.* FROBISHER
re-enters, still coughing, followed by BEATRICE.

FROBISHER. Your majesty, your majesty, did you pronounce? I
pray you, repeat yourself.

BEATRICE *and* FROBISHER *are kneeling at her feet. She says
nothing. They look up.*

ELIZABETH. They said, Elizabeth, you will never ride such a
great golden beast as that, what at your age, nine year old,
what a thing, and yet I stamped my foot and made such
threats that they set me up upon him some sixteen hands
high and though the muscle of him was strong and supple,
yet when I did ride him, he knew my strength and so
submitted as I rode him thrice around the courtyard and
back to the startled faces and said: 'Now. Now is he gentle
and I am gentle too. We may inside and pray.'

She closes her eyes and sleeps.

FROBISHER. Your majesty. Your majesty?

Blackout.

Scene Four
THE GHOST

A graveyard, near midnight. It's very dark. LUCIUS *comes on.*

LUCIUS. Which row did we bury the bugger in? It was summer
daylight when we stuck him under. Now it's poxy February
and too dark to read the names. Thought I'd recognise the
twinkling bluebells and the curiously named neighbour.
Scadge was it? Roderick Scadge, something like that.

He stumbles.

Oh Jesus. I don't think this is right at all. Should have asked
your man for something to see in the dark. The chimes'll be
on us in a moment and then –

He stumbles again.

A lingering pox on the nettle-mongering sexton, I'll never
find him now.

He pauses, then inspects the headstone where he has tripped.

'When I stood up, my lies provoked your mirth
Now you stand up while I lie i' the earth.'
Hieronymous Bodkin, fool.

A clock begins to strike midnight.

Not a moment too soon. Where's the bloody potion?

He delves into his jerkin, finds the potion, struggles with the stopper.

Come on, come on.

He gets the stopper off.

Nine. Ten. Eleven.

*He throws the potion over the grave and backs off, shielding his eyes.
For a long moment nothing happens, then there's a voice.*

VOICE. Over here, son.

>HIERONYMOUS BODKIN *appears in a strange light. On his
shoulder is a large, decapitated hawk. The head is tucked under the
bird's wing.* HIERONYMOUS *goes straight into his routine.*

HIERONYMOUS. There's this Spaniard, see, comes to
London, thinks he's a real Jack the Lad, walking over
London Bridge he passes this doxy –

LUCIUS. Dad –

HIERONYMOUS. – tits out here somewhere, so Pedro thinks
to himself, could be in there, know what I mean, know what I
mean –

LUCIUS. Dad, I don't want your act.

HIERONYMOUS. No bugger does these days. Don't talk to me
about getting bookings, purgatory. No seriously, he turns to
her and says: 'Hello darling, what d'you think to me three
foot ruff?' And she says –

LUCIUS. Dad, I want advice.

HIERONYMOUS. Oh Christ. Go on then.

LUCIUS. I'm at the crossroads of my career, I've got this
booking –

HIERONYMOUS. I know, I know, you think I don't know that,
I keep in touch.

LUCIUS. Sorry.

HIERONYMOUS. Your brother, Christ knows what he'll do on his own, about as funny as a rusty thumbscrew.

LUCIUS. There's something not quite right about it. It's like –

HIERONYMOUS. Yes?

LUCIUS. That slave girl. She tried to warn me off. I always respected you. Is this the right thing for me to do?

HIERONYMOUS. Can't say I like the act myself. But then, my old man didn't like my act either. Kept on trying to teach me his imitation of Henry the Seventh, I said no one's interested in Henry the –

LUCIUS. I don't mean is it funny. I know it's funny. I mean, is it safe?

HIERONYMOUS. Safe? You want to be funny *and* safe. Christ son, you know what you're asking for, you're asking for the poxy moon.

He advances on LUCIUS.

Look. See this. A brand. One of three impressed on my skin by the Queen's gaolers. See this. A dagger wound, second house at the Boar's Head, Blackfriars. Some mad Anabaptist reckoned I was taking the piss out of the Old Testament. I could go on. The poignards, the vicious knees in alleyways, the thundermugs emptied in my face. But I made them laugh. Sometimes the bastards hated me, but even while they thrust their rapiers in my gizzard, their teeth would dance a smile to my music. I fulfilled the contract of my profession. Our profession. I made them laugh. Through storm and hurricano, through fire and brimstone, at the moment the battleaxe was whistling towards the neck, I would set the giggling gums in motion. It is your mystery. There are only three pieces of advice I will ever give you: never apologise; never refuse money; and stick to your mystery. Stick to your bloody mystery or you will fall into limbo like a screaming soul. Do you understand?

LUCIUS. Yes.

HIERONYMOUS. Then I'll be off. Would you like to hear my bird sing before you go?

LUCIUS. Sing. Can he?

HIERONYMOUS. Oh yes. A sweet voice, a little disembodied,
   but a sweet voice.

HIERONYMOUS *sings*.

> Dost thou know the price of wheat
> Oh my fair young lady
> Canst thou say how I may eat
> Oh my bonny lady?

The HAWK *joins in, taking a higher part.*

> Canst thou ever say for sure
> When the raindrops next will pour
> When the wolf will reach your door
> Lady, lady?

> Canst thou know the price of corn
> Oh my white-haired lady
> Canst thou say why I was born
> Oh my sainted lady?

HIERONYMOUS *begins to fade from view.*

You must make them die. You must make them die laughing.

He's gone. LUCIUS *is alone.*

LUCIUS. And so I will go to it.
   This ghost to me hath been both kith and kin
   Whilst I draw breath, I'll strive to make them grin.

Blackout.

Scene Five
THE POLITICIAN

A courtyard in the open air by the river.
WARBURTON *is alone.*

WARBURTON. How this stale reign drags on and on: while we
   Her ministers who wait for power, must rust in all
   The footling offices of state. Our every deed
   Is double checked by Her on high who wields
   Her royal sceptre like a goad, chivying
   Her ministers as some stern schoolmarm snapping
   At her brood. We are but shadows thrown up
   By her sun, waxing sudden into strange and

Monstrous forms, then dwindling at her whim
To furtive shapes, scarce visible.
Her reign like Gaul has split into three parts:
The first saw devastation in the land,
The crops grown sick, the people wandering
In search of food and work. Then followed on
A time of seeming richness when merchants,
Making dizzy sums from picking fleas off
One another's backs, held sway, though all
The while the people muttered blood. Now
Stand we in the third and final phase,
Where she sits shakily in dwindling power,
None contradicting her through force of habit,
But plotting all the while their new estate
After her death. In these pale dog day times
Am I determined to prove a villain. One who
Waits not for the wheel to turn, but needs
Must push it till it runs at my own pace.
And in her time of sickness will I strike
To make the cards of state fall how I like.

FROBISHER *walks across the stage, perhaps conversing with*
secretaries.

WARBURTON. There's Frobisher, the ancient, trusty servant,
   Proving the adage that the dog will ape
   His mistress's behaviour. Him will I have
   Upon the hip in civil brawl, unmourned.

FROBISHER *goes off. From the other side of the stage,*
DAVENPORT *appears, carrying a rose, accompanied by a*
courtesan.

WARBURTON. Then Davenport, a most venereal man:
   One who leads the Cath'lic sect and waits
   His chance to turn the kingdom round. He,
   With his hot-head followers I'll embroil in
   Publick squall. So he goes to't.

DAVENPORT *goes off. From another part of the stage,* BEATRICE
leads on THE BISHOP, *an elderly, imposing figure.*

WARBURTON. And last this Bishop, led here by my daughter's
   Hand. Affecting much to disaffect the
   Reign, yet do his stocks and bonds grow well.
   Seeming to disapprove of licence and immoral acts,

Yet grows he fat on rents gained from the stews
  And brothels in the Clink which are a portion
Of his see. For this old hypocrite
I'll shape an end which suits his double face.

WARBURTON raises his shield. Suddenly ZANDA rushes at him from off-stage with a lance, lunging at him. He fends the lance off with the shield.

WARBURTON. Ha!

They both laugh.

Again!

ZANDA goes off, then rushes back again with the lance. WARBURTON parries again and the lance shatters. ZANDA sits, exhausted.

Enough. You should have seen me in my youth. At the Accession Day tilts, I could hold my own against all comers.

ZANDA. All?

WARBURTON. All but two or three. You make a fine charger.

ZANDA. I am used to bits and bridles.

WARBURTON. Perhaps too used.

ZANDA. My Lord?

WARBURTON. It may be time for me to set you free.

Pause.

ZANDA. Why should you do that? You bought me as a slave. I am your thing. Men do not give away their things.

WARBURTON. Except for a price.

ZANDA. You would sell me to someone else?

WARBURTON. No. To yourself.

ZANDA. Explain.

WARBURTON. We're living in a time of change. The prizes of state will be won by decisive action. Not too early, not too late. I am the man who is in tune with the times. The crucial phase is upon us. You have a part to play. There are risks. If you succeed, I will hand over the key to your chains.

ZANDA. My freedom?

WARBURTON. Yes.

ZANDA. And what part must I play?

WARBURTON. There is a Lord who loves you, Davenport, the
    Catholic's guiding light.

ZANDA. You call that love? He treats me like his horse.

WARBURTON. He is an English gentleman, that's love.

ZANDA. I have been shy of him of late.

WARBURTON. Then he'll be keen to use his spurs. You must
    encourage him.

ZANDA. But that's not all.

WARBURTON. No. He is ambitious. For himself. For his
    beliefs. He still hopes the Infanta of Spain may succeed and
    return England to popery. If he sensed he had support, he
    would attempt a coup.

ZANDA. Which must fail.

WARBURTON. Which must fail and leave me stronger.

ZANDA. But there will be no support.

WARBURTON. Not yet. There are in London thirty thousand
    souls who walk the streets with no lodging and little hope of
    food.

    We hear the rattle of chains in the background.

    The poor. The dispossessed. The mad. Those who have
    nothing to lose. All of them have felt Elizabeth's lash. Half of
    them would storm the tower for a bowl of soup. You have
    some power among them.

ZANDA. I drink with the highest and the lowest.

WARBURTON. Very well then. Make the sap rise in Davenport.
    Lead him to the mob. Present him as their leader. If they rise
    in riot, you shall have your key.

    Pause.

ZANDA. And what then?

    Pause.

    Where would I go? I was conveyed a thousand miles to be
    your slave. What would I do if you unlocked my chains? Walk

back towards the sun? My home is long forgot. But if I stayed
in England which way would I turn to make a living? Become
a fairground show among the legless and the double sexed?
Or decorate the beds of ancient merchants with a taste for
skin?

WARBURTON. I would provide for you.

ZANDA. How much? I play your game, I must know the stakes.

WARBURTON. If I make my game, the chain of office gleams
on my collar. There is nothing I could not do for you.

ZANDA. What, make me a lady who paints her face and rides a
carriage to the park?

WARBURTON. If I gain power you would name your price.

ZANDA. And if you lose?

WARBURTON. A ship sinks with all hands. Each man fights for
his own barrel.

ZANDA. I will speak with Davenport. And make soundings with
the mob.

WARBURTON. Why, there's my steed!

ZANDA *suddenly picks up the broken spear and thrusts, half
playfully at* WARBURTON. *He parries with the shield, laughing.*

ZANDA. Why, there's your slave.

WARBURTON. And here's my daughter with my prelate. Fetch
some wine. Then watch and hold your tongue.

THE BISHOP *comes on, led by* BEATRICE. ZANDA *curtsies,
then goes off.*

THE BISHOP. Tuppence now to cross the river! Those
ferrymen want shooting.

WARBURTON. It's private enterprise.

THE BISHOP. It's a cartel. The crown's too stingy to build
another bridge so we're all at the mercy of a lot of browned
off matelots who've sat on their arses doing sweet naff-all
since the Armada. And their conversation! I wouldn't mind
paying twopence if the bastards would shut up. All they do is
rabbit on about how they navigated for Francis Drake. Most
of them couldn't find their way to Lambeth in a flat-
bottomed punt.

WARBURTON. Tisk, tisk.

THE BISHOP. Then they want a free blessing. Bastards!

WARBURTON. But what can you do? The water belongs to everybody, you can't privatise it.

BEATRICE. Sit down, your Grace.

THE BISHOP. There's something wrong somewhere.

> THE BISHOP *sits.* ZANDA *come on with three glasses of wine. She distributes them, then goes off to the side of the stage looking out, apart from the scene.*

WARBURTON. My daughter saw the Queen yesterday.

THE BISHOP. And?

BEATRICE. She's very near the end. And she still hasn't pronounced. Frobisher is out of his mind with worry. He's started bringing in the alchemists.

THE BISHOP. Little creep. About his level.

BEATRICE. They want her to say James.

THE BISHOP. Sanctimonious Scotch git. I suppose you can't blame him. Bands of long-nosed Presbyterians stuffing their medicine down your throat when you're still learning to crawl, bound to have some effect.

BEATRICE. She's hanging on to the very end before she names a successor. She wants to keep the mystique of the reign going until she drops.

THE BISHOP. And there's that appalling little twerp Frobisher trying to look like the man in charge, the one who's got the keys to the till.

WARBURTON. Exactly, so when James comes to London, Frobisher'll keep his place. We can't have that. We have to set the agenda. Fast. Look what will happen. James doesn't even approve of smoking. He'll take one look at the Liberty of the Clink and close the lot down.

THE BISHOP. The City won't stand for that. Work hard, play hard, those boys need their drugs. And they'll be calling the tune. Parliament's given the Queen an easy passage because they're frightened of her. But they're just biding their time. They'll give James three months to strut around, then they'll cut his purse strings and leave him begging.

WARBURTON. Exactly. He'll be a king without substance. So he'll have to compensate with style. And his style will be cold and dismal like Tuesday's mutton. He won't care if all the merchants and bankers are rogering themselves stupid and sucking smoke up their noses on the south bank *as long as he can't see it.*

THE BISHOP. I hope you're right. My see can't operate without the money we draw from the Southwark stews. I've got six hundred clergy who eat and drink the profits of whoring. I couldn't go back to supporting them on industry, we've cut back too much.

BEATRICE. So the emphasis is on style. Do the houses up. Some nice curtains. Sober signs to hang at the windows. Perhaps little psalm books for the girls to carry in public.

WARBURTON. But most important, you have to go on the record. The Scots put great faith in the written word. Preach a sermon backing the new morality and publish it as a pamphlet. Nice, sent;entious title, distribute it to the right people. The moral high ground, that's where you have to be.

THE BISHOP. It's a thought.

WARBURTON. And maybe a couple of glancing blows at the Catholics wouldn't come amiss. There's talk of a last throw to get the Infanta on the throne. Something hard-line, determinist would look good.

THE BISHOP. I'll take a glance at my old University notes.

WARBURTON. That's the style. And make it soon. The next few days will be crucial. If we don't get a grip quickly, Frobisher will be in and we'll all have to retire to the country.

THE BISHOP. How do we unseat him?

WARBURTON. The plan is under way. Just sit back and watch. It's best if you know nothing. You're a man of God.

THE BISHOP. My trust is in you.

THE BISHOP *gets up to go. He shakes* WARBURTON*'s hand. Tableau.*

LUCIUS *comes on.* ZANDA *intercepts him.*

LUCIUS. Mistress Zanda. What make you here?

ZANDA. I am the stone animal that sits at the foot of the statue.

LUCIUS. Then you'll not bite.

She makes mock roaring noises.

The Minister is a statue?

ZANDA. A very old and haughty one. He squats atop a pinnacle and the world tramps to do obeisance at the foot of his column.

LUCIUS. Save for the things that fly –

ZANDA. – and they do shower their favour from above.

They both laugh.

ZANDA. I warned you to stay away, fool

LUCIUS. I took advice from higher up.

ZANDA. And what do you want here?

LUCIUS. I've been sent for.

ZANDA. Perhaps then, you are one who comes to the monument with a swab and bucket after the autumn flocks have flown.

LUCIUS. It is a worthy mystery.

On the other side of the stage, the tableau breaks. BEATRICE *leads the* BISHOP *off.*

WARBURTON. Zanda!

ZANDA. The stone speaks.

WARBURTON. Is this your fool?

ZANDA. Fool enough, but none of mine.

LUCIUS. Lucius Bodkin, your eminence.

WARBURTON *drinks and looks* LUCIUS *up and down.*

WARBURTON. A scurvy fellow enough. My daughter Beatrice speaks well of your canting.

LUCIUS. I cant.

WARBURTON. These Dutch fellows. You know the Dutch do you?

LUCIUS. I've queued behind them in bars.

WARBURTON. Why then, you know them. But let me advise

you further. It would well benefit us all if this, our feast went
on so merrily that in future times, men held their sides and
groaned as they recalled the jests they heard. Commerce is
the great wheel of the world, but still the wheel needs oil –
you are that sickly liquid, and I bid you, when you are put
upon, to pour as thick as plumtree gum upon the heads of
those that heed you. Your Dutchman is an uncommon good
fellow – one that likes well a jest told hard against himself:
and these, that I will tell you, are the chiefest butts for quips
and quiddities that any can devise.

WARBURTON *stands, almost performing.* LUCIUS *and* ZANDA
sit on the floor. BEATRICE *returns, watching from a distance.*

First likes the Dutchman well a jest upon his tongue. For is
there a man in Europe that, unborn to't, can make more of
the Lowland drawl then of two seals honking in a bucket at a
Whitsun fair? Did not the Emperor Charles call it the very
speech of horses? So hold not back, but pitch in straight and
make fair imitation of our guests with such as 'Neeeighhh'
and 'Whooaah' or any counterfeiting of the equine bray as
shall best seem to fit the moment and they are yours to
fashion how you will.

LUCIUS *and* ZANDA *are appreciative.*

Next loves your Dutchman well a pleasantry upon his greed
for gold, his lust for money and his endless avarice. For it is
but to begin with: 'Fellows were there three, one French, one
English true and one of Amsterdam' for them to know the
point and very seamark of the jest will be their merchant
disposition and their graspingness. Such canting, sure, will
set the table on a roar as each fair dart, well-aimed, gouges
out their blank and buttery eyes.

WARBURTON *pauses again for* LUCIUS *and* ZANDA's
laughter. BEATRICE *watches, cooler.*

Last, but by no means backward in this sport, your
Dutchman relishes some ribbing of his meagre history; for lo,
the nation is but young, a mewling infant, where we are
grown to sturdy manhood. And so, such few heroic men as
have been thrown up by their tide are objects all for fond
deriding and unseemly pranks. But chiefest of these, the
braggart William of Orange, he who led the Butterballs – so
must you call them – in their Great Revolt is, in their
pastime, now a target for much scorn and scoffing mirth.

Why, mention but the very fruit – I mean the orange – to
your Hollander in slighting context and he will straight be
falling on the floor, his overshirt stuffed tight into his mouth
while from his eyes course tears of pent up joy unleashed by
helpless ululation.

ZANDA *and* LUCIUS *applaud.*

These are your targets: set your arrows fair
And laughter's garlands will adorn your hair.

LUCIUS. I'm surprised you're not doing the turn yourself.

WARBURTON. Parliament now is stage enough for me, but yet
when I was young . . . enough of that.

LUCIUS. But what about Spanish jokes. They're the thing at
the moment –

WARBURTON. No.

LUCIUS. There's this one about a Dago with a three foot ruff
who –

WARBURTON. No. Nothing touching your Iberian. It will not
serve. Your Hollander is your butt, him and him alone.

LUCIUS. I am your servant.

WARBURTON. In all things be you so.

LUCIUS. Your precepts will I harbour in my thought:
For but one laugh, I set the world at naught.

WARBURTON *claps a hand around* LUCIUS*'s shoulder and
escorts him to the door.*

Farewell, your eminence.

WARBURTON. Farewell, good Lucius, till Wednesday next.

LUCIUS *goes.*

The fool is primed, the primate fooled. Our plot works on.

BEATRICE. Will not the anger of the Dutchman at this fool
rebound on us?

WARBURTON. They'll see him as a Catholic impostor, friend
to the revolt. When we smash the Infanta's mob, we smash
the naughty fool and our credit with the Dutch will soar.
More wine.

ZANDA *pours.*

My daughter, there are plans for you as well.

BEATRICE *approaches a little suspiciously.* ZANDA *looks on.*

In the past I have made matches for you.

BEATRICE. No more of that.

WARBURTON. And you have turned them down.

BEATRICE. Sometimes. The Queen has always shown displeasure at the thought of losing me.

WARBURTON. She'll die before the winter's out. Then where will you be? James will need pikemen more than ladies-in-waiting.

BEATRICE. There's time to consider –

WARBURTON. There is no time. You're past the age a father should maintain you. Each day we wait, your dowry rises. The better matches have been lost to girls who didn't seek to frighten off a husband. Your nature is too dominant, you make men fearful.

BEATRICE. I have no need of fearful men.

WARBURTON. You need a man as fast as I can get you one. Affairs of state will soon consume me utterly. I mean to marry you now and get you off my hands. I have a good offer which I would accept.

BEATRICE. Who?

WARBURTON. A family that would settle well with ours. Their standing in the country and their breeding will be fair exchange for our hold on power and our city fame –

BEATRICE. Who?

WARBURTON. The dowry they are asking would be –

BEATRICE *picks up the broken spear and threatens* WARBURTON.

BEATRICE. Who?

WARBURTON. This show of rage will gain you nothing.

BEATRICE. This is no show of rage, this is the very stuff.

WARBURTON. Put down your weapon and I'll speak.

BEATRICE. You'll speak of husbands first before we talk of weapons.

Pause.

WARBURTON. A young man called Martin Gridling, a most worthy fellow –

BEATRICE. Gridling!

WARBURTON. Whose reputation ranks him –

BEATRICE. Ranks him as a stickleback among bright salmon. A clod of clay, a sprouting boil, a meal of steam at a banquet. You would marry me to him!

WARBURTON. I gained you preferment at court until I won for you the pride of place amongst the Queen's women. These times now are past – not of my choosing – and we now must make new plans –

BEATRICE. You sought to thrust me forward at the court so I could be your intelligencer there, in places where no man could venture. I grew in power through my own virtues not through your push. You gained from knowledge of the Queen's bedchamber thoughts, her hairbrush confidences, and now you seek to throw me off –

WARBURTON. There is no seeking here. There is command, there is obedience. I negotiate with cardinals and princes not with my own flesh. The match is set. The time alone awaits. The queen's obsequies will be your wedding banns.

BEATRICE *hurls the spear in the direction of* WARBURTON's *departing back, but it fails to carry. She turns to* ZANDA.

BEATRICE. Do you know this man, this Gridling?

ZANDA. No, my lady.

BEATRICE. The litter's runt, a streaming nostril. He succeeds to the estate because his elder brothers died in honest brawls. He, lacking education, wit and strength is one who loiters in the town, aping the manners of the day. He now affects the roaring persuasion, smoking, being gulled at cards and seeking quarrels with the passing crowd on Ludgate Hill.

ZANDA. Then you must not have him, he is none for you.

BEATRICE. My father's mind is settled.

ZANDA. How far are you prepared to go?

BEATRICE *looks at her.*

ZANDA. What would you do to resist this match?

ZANDA *picks up the broken spear and the shield, holding them by her side.*

Rail and play the schoolgirl, simper and stamp your foot but in the end comply? Or yet the woman's part, do what you're told, yet keep the better half of you aloof, injuring your husband where it never shows, but with each blow confounding your own nature?

BEATRICE. What would you do?

ZANDA *assumes a warlike attitude with the spear and shield.*

ZANDA. I would play the man. Cunning and conspiracy are the virtues of the age. These you must employ, and what is more, the ruthlessness to see them to the end. Don't brood upon a wrong for forty years. Out with your weapon, cut off the offending part. This Gridling must be trimmed.

BEATRICE. My guilt will seem too obvious –

ZANDA. That is the place of cunning. To lay the guilt of crime at some other's door. Leave this part to me. If Master Gridling would seek to be a roarer, I'll give him reason enough to roar till Doomsday.

She hands BEATRICE *the spear.*

Show me your mettle.

ZANDA *holds up the shield.* BEATRICE *thrusts in the spear. It quivers.*

ZANDA. Why, that's my lady.

Blackout.

Scene Six
THE HERMITS

By the Thames, very late at night. The ABRAHAM MEN *come on. They are vagrants who simulate madness in order to gain sympathy and money. Some simulate palsy as well. Occasionally they dance and sing. They're dressed in rags and chains and carry begging tins.*

ABRAHAM MEN. We who were the forgotten
Are now become unforgettable
We who were the leprous sick
Are now become the perfectible
We who were sores on the body politic
The Commonweal turned rotten
The plaguey, the manic, the lunar lunatic
The underworld of misbegotten
Now stand upright in our Bedlam buskins
Waving our chains on high
And you who ignored us on the bridge of skulls
Are now condemned to die.

The ABRAHAM MEN *raise their chains and wave them above their heads. They advance angrily forward towards the audience, but do not reach them.*

ZANDA *comes on with a silver pistol in her hand. She is wearing a cloak. She fires a shot above her head. Immediately the* ABRAHAM MEN *come to heel like a pack of trained dogs. They cluster around* ZANDA. *She distributes crusts of bread to them.*

ZANDA. Back into the shadows.

The ABRAHAM MEN *slink back into the shadows.* ZANDA *merges in among them. The river seethes and splashes.*

DAVENPORT *comes on. He is edgy, looking for someone. Silence. Then, suddenly a laugh.* DAVENPORT *draws his sword. Immediately,* ZANDA *comes on from the opposite direction. She stands, wrapped in a cloak. She watches* DAVENPORT's *back as she searches round for an invisible enemy. Then he senses her and whirls round.*

ZANDA. What, Sir Richard Davenport, in this degraded spot with his rapier out?

DAVENPORT. There was a noise. Over there.

ZANDA. The river.

DAVENPORT. Human noises. A laugh.

ZANDA. The river is human, composed of human flux: our daily deaths, our pissings and our bloody courses. In Cordoba, stone statues move at mention of Our Lady: in London, the river laughs. Trust me.

DAVENPORT. You speak of Spain: this has a meaning?

ZANDA. It is a place I have visited.

DAVENPORT. With chains around your ankles. Is this called visiting?

ZANDA. My dress was something metallic: I aped the spirit of the age.

DAVENPORT. The Infanta is in arms: her powers and her intelligences wait on your report. What's happening in the palace?

ZANDA. Too little eating of fruit.

DAVENPORT. You shall not sport with me in this.

ZANDA. I do not sport. I say there is too little fruit. When you yourself hath ploughed the waves as cargo, then know you well all other cargoes: coal and iron and food. To London sails but little fruit: even in the court, the people don't eat it and so they are become melancholic of mood, much given to secrecy and prey to mad, fantastic plotting. For this disease, there are two cures: one is to knife your neighbour's gizzard, the other is to eat more oranges. In London, the first course is preferred.

DAVENPORT walks towards her.

DAVENPORT. And yet, I'll make you speak, my soft intelligencer.

She turns her back on him. He grasps her waist and kisses the back of her neck. She enjoys this in a detached way.

You should be afraid to turn your back on me.

ZANDA. The Dutch delegation will be received tomorrow evening. They dine at six. Afterwards there will be entertainment in the Golden Chamber. My lady has employed a fool whose ravings will occasion great displeasure in our guests. He is one of the new kind, dispos'd to railing at company and holding up the manners of his audience to his outstretched tongue. The Dutch will take this as discourtesy and draw their swords. I will arrange for the extinguishing of certain tapers, and in the darkness and confusion, our enemy will undergo the swift divorce of body and soul.

DAVENPORT. What of the fool?

ZANDA. He is a fool, your Dutchman's sword is sharp – in short he will go to't.

DAVENPORT. Poor fool.

ZANDA. This death will be the sign for your revolt. You Catholics must rise up with whatever power you can command –

DAVENPORT. It cannot be! Our number in London is not sufficient. If you could hold your hand three weeks, we would have an army –

ZANDA. In three weeks, James will be on the throne. It must be now.

DAVENPORT. Many people will die.

DAVENPORT becomes more passionate. She encourages him, though her back is still turned.

ZANDA. The soul is coupled with the body. I have known many couplings of this sort. A little spark of spirit, but one small spurt. The coming together is of no significance, nor is the moment when they're thrust apart.

DAVENPORT. This rebellion will come too soon. My power will be weak against Elizabeth's iron guard.

Suddenly ZANDA pushes DAVENPORT away. She makes a low whistle. Instantly, the ABRAHAM MEN appear, completely encircling DAVENPORT.

DAVENPORT. You have ensnared me.

ZANDA. No. This is your army. You're right. A few Catholic nobles is not sufficient force to overturn the peace of London. To gain true power, you must embrace the mob. These wretched creatures have nothing to lose and will fight with more desperation than your well-heeled friends. But beware – they trust you now and have their expectations. If you should fail them, it will be your throat.

The ABRAHAM MEN begin to clink their chains against their begging tins.

DAVENPORT. I am a Catholic nobleman, I cannot lead this mob.

ZANDA. Then they must needs lead you.

The ABRAHAM MEN descend on DAVENPORT. They surround

him, tear off his fine clothes, force him onto his knees and blindfold him. They tie his hands behind his back. ZANDA takes his sword. The clinking rises to a crescendo, then cuts out suddenly. ZANDA flicks the sword noisily in the air around DAVENPORT. At each cut of the sword, the ABRAHAM MEN rattle their chains. Finally, in complete silence, ZANDA makes a tiny cut on DAVENPORT's chest. DAVENPORT gasps. ZANDA throws down the sword, kneels by DAVENPORT and licks blood from his wound.

ZANDA. Now, my fine Davenport, we have sworn this matter in blood. You are the general and this is your army. The uprising will go ahead as I demanded. I will come to your bedchamber tonight where we may plot in detail. But for now, these people have nothing and you have so very much.

She turns to the ABRAHAM MEN.

Share his pelf.

The ABRAHAM MEN descend on DAVENPORT's clothes and money. Each one grabs some part of his property. They line up behind him.

ZANDA. So. Sir Richard Davenport, you have spread your mortal goods among these men. They have become you. You have become them.

The ABRAHAM MEN laugh, then slowly disappear in different directions clanking their chains.

ZANDA watches them, then puts down the sword in front of him. Slowly she takes a small orange from within the folds of her cloak. She puts it in his mouth and clamps his teeth on it.

ZANDA. Till tonight, I will not fail your bed, nor you my army.

She goes. DAVENPORT makes desperate noises. Silence. Then the OLD WOMAN comes on. She sees DAVENPORT. Stops. Removes the orange. Hides it in the folds of her dress. Goes off.

DAVENPORT. You're there. I know you're still there.

Blackout.

Scene Seven
THE SERMON

THE BISHOP *preaches. During the opening text,* ELIZABETH

slowly comes out of her trance and starts reading from a small, bound pamphlet. This is the text of THE BISHOP*'s sermon.*

THE BISHOP. 'Let every soul be subject unto the higher powers, for there is no power but of God, and the powers that be are ordained of God.'

Thus speaks the Apostle Paul to the Romans. I am no Apostle, no more are you Romans. But I speak unto you in the same wise and to the same purpose. What is the authority of Kings and Queens and whence does it flow? It is the authority on which our kingdom is founded, and it flows from God. And just as God rules absolutely in the heavens and in the firmament, so do princes in their earthly domain hold sway. For insofar as Lucifer, the most shining creature of God, rebelled and became the foulest fiend in the black pit of hopelessness, so too does the rebel against King, Prince or Minister become cast down into the pits and chasms of our earthly desponds.

Yet there be some, so loose in their affairs they wait not for the hand of God to cast them into hell, nor yet for the strong arm of the law to throw them into prison, but do of their own will give themselves up to the yoke of servitude and cast themselves into darkness by their own doing, whether by gaming, drabbing, pickpocketing, brawling, taking of tobacco or swearing against God. And none more so than those that do frequent the place called the Liberty of the Clink, than which there is no greater paradox, for what is less at liberty than a soul fettered to such a place – where daily may be seen the lowest women consorting with the most abject and unreputable of men.

For mistake not, ye shall be judged by your rebellion, and whether it be rebellion against God, or against King, or against good and righteous conduct through the passage of your earthly life, ye shall be cast into the sulphurous pit. By one great test shall ye be judged by God – by your obedience to his Almighty power; to the terrestrial power of his princes; and to His written statutes of earthly conduct.

It is written: 'a wise and righteous king makes his realm and people wealthy' and happy is the land wherein such subjects dwell. But how, sayeth the unwise, if the case be contrary? Is it not written: 'A foolish prince destroys the people and a covetous king undoes his subjects.' Should not the subject then seek to overthrow his king?

This is the reasoning of the fool: for shall it be that the servant shall make judgement upon the master: that the child shall lead the father, that the foot shall rule the head? It is a manifest absurdity. For when the subjects shall come to judge the king, what perilous times must of necessity ensue.

In all things order, in all dealings sobriety and in all matters obedience.

THE BISHOP *crosses himself. Some plainsong is heard. Then, suddenly,* ELIZABETH *hurls the text of the sermon onto the floor. The plainsong stops in mid note.* THE BISHOP, *startled, stares out front and falls on his knees.*

ELIZABETH *looks out front, not at* THE BISHOP.

ELIZABETH. This sermon you have spoke and published –

THE BISHOP. Your majesty –

ELIZABETH. It is a clarion call to plotting and unrest –

THE BISHOP. My text was obedience to the crown in the face of rebellion.

ELIZABETH. What rebellion?

THE BISHOP. Why, any rebellion that would unseat your majesty.

ELIZABETH. Why do you preach rebellion?

THE BISHOP. I preach not rebellion –

ELIZABETH. Why even speak of rebellion? Who rebels?

THE BISHOP. None that I know –

ELIZABETH. Then this is code and cypher and no plain dealing. To rail against a sin that none commits? As one who would prevail upon the unicorn to pick no pockets or beard the gryphon for his usury? There is a double meaning here. To entreat submissive people not to rebel? Why, they will read this text another way and think: 'He speaks of things he would much like to see. He means us to take swords against the crown.'

THE BISHOP. My theme was only God and the sovereign's right divine.

ELIZABETH. Which things are not at issue. A secret purpose shows itself in this. Those who would confront strong rule do not speak openly, they dissemble with circuitous tongues, and, mouthing thoughts that all hold to be true, condemn those very precepts into doubt. He who says: 'The crossbeams of the house are strong and bear a mighty load' is calling straight for saws and axes.

THE BISHOP. I praised the house, not its destruction.

ELIZABETH. And spoke you also of tobacco?

THE BISHOP. Your majesty, I did, it is a most pestilent and –

ELIZABETH. Meaning our cousin James –

THE BISHOP. Upon my life, I do deny it –

ELIZABETH. For it is known that he hath sworn strong terms against the smoking of this weed, and but to say the word 'tobacco' is to invoke his presence.

THE BISHOP. I but condemned the looseness of the merchants who infest the Liberty of the Clink, and rot with their damp souls the ship of state.

ELIZABETH. And in the Clink, which Bishop stands as shepherd to these souls?

THE BISHOP. Why, I – I –

ELIZABETH. And this confirms it home. A politicking Pastor I abhor. Your duty is to show your flock the way to heaven, not meddle in affairs of state.

THE BISHOP. In all things, I only sought to –

ELIZABETH. On your feet.

THE BISHOP *stands.*

I would have you make better acquaintance of the souls within your see. And to this end, I consign you, while a proper charge is made, to spend your leisure in the Clink – not in its stews or inns, but in the gaol whose key you hold.

THE BISHOP. To my own prison?

ELIZABETH. The Clink. It pleases me. Away!

The lights on THE BISHOP *go out.*

ELIZABETH *stares ahead.*

Thus, all of a sudden, will she flare into a mighty blaze, and then, as quickly as she tinder'd, dwindle to a plume of smoke, wrapping itself around the thought of sleep, but not quite going out.

ELIZABETH *subsides into her former state.*

Blackout.

Scene Eight
THE DELEGATION

The entertainment for the DUTCH TRADE DELEGATION. *A lutanist plays discreetly on a small raised area. The whole company except the* FROBISHER *and* LUCIUS *actors play the* DUTCH TRADE DELEGATION. *They are dressed uniformly – perhaps voluminous black cloaks and steeple hats – alternatively as business executives of the 1990s. They sit on a long wooden bench with their backs to the audience. When the lutanist finishes playing, the* DUTCH *applaud by hammering their feet on the ground.*

FROBISHER *comes forward and stands on the raised area.*

FROBISHER. My friends. We are entering an historic period of co-operation between our two countries. Though in the past, there have been differences and misunderstandings, we are now travelling the same road together: the road that leads to a peaceful Protestant Europe with massive trading opportunities in a free, competitive and ever-expanding market.

The DUTCH *stamp their feet in approval.*

Needless to say, this aim is not being pursued in every European capital. The Spanish threat is everywhere. All I will say on that subject at the moment is this: we in London know who our friends are.

The DUTCH *stamp again.*

Gentlemen. I wish you a successful business trip and a pleasant stay in London.

All drink heartily.

Later we will be enjoying a masque and a Burgomaster's dance. But now, a fool with a rapidly growing reputation, Master Lucius Bodkin.

The DUTCH *stamp and shuffle.* FROBISHER *goes and sits*

among them. LUCIUS *comes onto the stage. He carries the skull we saw in the audition scene.*

LUCIUS. Staying in London long are you? A week, did you say? It's long enough. (*Holds up skull.*) Two days. It's true. He only came over to sign a bill of lading. Last Tuesday it was. Gentleman over there doesn't believe me. No, not you, the one next to you in the big hat. Oh sorry, madam, no offence. Anyway, over here last week, now he looks like this. Prussian feller. Improved him, hasn't it? No, it's this plague we've been getting. Seriously. Lot of it about. They come round and paint a big blue cross on your door. Nice touch that. Woman lives next to me went out and got infected deliberately. She did. I said what you do that for, she said I've been living in this house thirty year and this is the first time that door's seen a lick. (*Pause.*) Thirty year. Never seen a lick. Blue paint.

He opens up the top of the skull. Dips in a spoon and starts drinking a black liquid from it.

Well that gruel wasn't filling was it? No, I'm only joking about the plague. They've got it under control, this government. No problem.

Suddenly, he starts swaying and retching. The 'pus' from the skull spatters the DUTCH TRADE DELEGATION.

Whoops, sorry. Sorry about that. No, I am, sir, gentleman next to you got twice your helping, there you go.

He spatters more 'pus'. The TRADE DELEGATION *are getting restless.* LUCIUS *decides to cut the rest of his plague gags and go straight into his Dutch material.*

No, it's a funny place Holland and no mistake. Been there have you? Sorry, course you have. I forget myself from time to time. Talk funny, don't they. Very strange. I was over there last year, I meet this bloke walking down the road, I say: 'Where am I?', he says: 'Utrecht'. I say: 'I know how I bloody got here', he says: 'That's the name of the place.' I say: 'Can you shut your horse up a minute, I can't hear a word you're saying.'

There is a definite rustle of disapproval. LUCIUS *is bewildered but sticks to his act.*

No, there's a Frenchman, an Englishman and a Dutchman. They decide to open a tavern. A tavern. They want it to look

marvellous, very chic, the latest thing, covers on the seats.
The Frenchman says: 'Ah want zeez seatz covered in zee
finest French lace.' The Englishman says: 'I want these seats
covered in the finest English wool'. The Dutchman says: 'I
want these seats covered in arses.' (*Pause.*) Arses.

*A bread roll bounces off his head. He carries on gamely. He gets three
oranges out of his jerkin and starts juggling with them.*

No, no, don't knock it, it's difficult this bit. What's even
harder is, while you're doing it, you have to think of the
names of three famous Dutchmen.

The DUTCH *are on the verge of uproar.*

William of Orange? No, famous Dutchmen, not famous
greengrocers.

The DUTCH *are now in open revolt.* FROBISHER *tries to
intervene to prevent them storming the stage. Swords are drawn.*
FROBISHER *is stabbed. Suddenly all the lights go out. Some
confused noises.*

VOICES. Lights! Bring in some lights!

Some tapers are brought in. FROBISHER *is lying dead on the
ground. Nobody moves.*

LUCIUS. Don't blame me. I mean, I was just up here doing my
act. It was one of you.

Nobody is sure what to do, but LUCIUS *has made up his mind to
escape.*

LUCIUS. I told you London was dangerous.

LUCIUS *makes a grab for* FROBISHER*'s body and props it up in
front of him.*

Honest, I didn't see anyone stab him. It's this bloody plague
if you ask me. It was something in the gruel I bet, we could
all have got it.

Some of the DUTCH *begin to laugh.*

It's no good laughing now, you sick bastards. This bloke was
something important, you'll never get to kiss the Queen's
feet now. And you can wave goodbye to all those fat contracts
you were expecting to sign. Haven't you lot been on one of
those management courses? The first thing they tell you is:
'Don't kill the host, he may not be able to buy anything from

you afterwards.'

The DUTCH *are in fits.*

But no, Ladies and Gentlemen, you really have been a marvellous audience, but we must go now, me, and my mate, another engagement to fulfil. So it's goodnight from me, Lucius Bodkin, and goodnight from him. It's the first time we've ever worked together as a double act, look out for us, we call ourselves, the quick and the dead. That's right, lady, I'm the quick one.

He manipulates FROBISHER's *hand.*

Bye-bye. Bye-bye.

The DUTCH *are now laughing hysterically.* LUCIUS *makes* FROBISHER *point to an imaginary figure behind the* DUTCH.

Look, he thinks he can see the murderer.

The DUTCH *all turn round to look. Instantly,* LUCIUS *makes off with* FROBISHER's *body over his shoulder. When the* DUTCH *notice he's gone, they are uncertain which way to give chase.*

Noise and alarums without. The GUARD *rushes on.*

GUARD. A plot! A plot is laid! The Catholics are in arms. The mob has risen with them. Show no mercy.

All draw swords and exit after the GUARD.

Blackout.

Interval.

Scene Nine
THE BODY

BUTLER's *shop.* BUTLER *is sitting at his table, inspecting a page of printed manuscript. A knock on the door.* BUTLER *looks around warily, hides the paper.*

BUTLER. Who is it?

LUCIUS. Let me in, it's urgent.

BUTLER *goes to the door, checks, opens it.* LUCIUS *comes in. He looks around furtively, making sure there's no one else there. He does this because he still has the body of* FROBISHER *across his shoulders.*

LUCIUS. You alone?

BUTLER. Jesus. Look, if this is the geezer you raised from the dead I don't want to know –

LUCIUS *flings* FROBISHER*'s body down on the table. The face stares at* BUTLER.

BUTLER. Jesus.

LUCIUS. Who was he?

BUTLER. Jesus!!

LUCIUS. Who was he?

BUTLER. Are you having me on?

LUCIUS. Last week. When I came here to buy the potion. He was here. Something important to do with the court.

BUTLER. He's well dead. Poor old John. You really don't know?

LUCIUS. I'm a fool, remember.

BUTLER. John Frobisher. Privy Councillor. Only the sovereign's first source of advice. Not the throne, just the power behind it.

LUCIUS. Frobisher.

BUTLER. How did he die?

LUCIUS. Stabbed. A mob of angry Dutchmen.

BUTLER. What circumstances?

LUCIUS. I was at the end of my act. It was all going wrong. I'd been misinformed. The Dutch Trade delegation – I was taking the piss out of them, they didn't like it –

BUTLER. You were taking the piss out of the Dutch? And *he* gets killed.

LUCIUS. I was set up. I don't know why. I only got away because I was holding on to him. I kept running. They meant me to die. He's my only clue.

BUTLER *has been casting a professional eye over the body.*

BUTLER. Venom. Venom on my life. Someone was making sure. Poor John. He was the only one to go down?

LUCIUS. Yes.

BUTLER. Venom. Look at his face. Foul play without a doubt.
Venom in the drink. Given personally. Probably someone he
trusted. Poison ring maybe. Lift the catch, let it loose. Well
dead. Venom. The stabbing was window dressing, see. Only
needed someone to sock him on the jaw and he'd have
pegged out.

Pause.

LUCIUS. What should I do?

BUTLER. Get out. Of here. Now. And take this lump of
nothing with you.

LUCIUS. But –

BUTLER. No buts. One of the most powerful men in London
gets killed and you want to leave him here? No dice. On your
way, my pretty fool. With your burden. Dump him. I
recommend Bear Street, the plague carts are in business
there and he'll be just one among many. Here.

BUTLER *paints a blue cross over the body.*

That should keep the nosy buggers away. Dump him. Then
run. Because you, my pretty fool, are the man in the adage
who has lived beyond his appointed hour.

LUCIUS *lifts the body back onto his shoulder. He heads for the door.
Turns.*

LUCIUS. Where should I go?

BUTLER. Scotland's quiet.

LUCIUS *goes.*

Blackout.

Scene Ten
THE COMMAND

ELIZABETH *on the throne.* WARBURTON *on his knees in front of
her, his forehead touching the floor.* ELIZABETH *is transformed, full
of awesome power.*

ELIZABETH. He was the one man I trusted. The man upon
whom I could rely. Killed in a brawl by a swinish herd of
Dutchmen.

WARBURTON *lifts his head to speak.*

Don't interrupt me!

His head goes back to the floor.

There's a bunch of left-footers roaming the streets inciting the vagrants to riot. And no one can tell me what's going on.

WARBURTON. The rebellion, your majesty, has been crushed and the ringleaders rounded –

ELIZABETH. Silence! And this fool. Sees it all. And makes off with Frobisher's body. The man was a privy councillor. If a privy councillor can't expect to get a Christian burial, where's the incentive for public service? Does anyone know where the body is?

Pause. WARBURTON *looks up warily and sees an answer is required.*

WARBURTON. Only the fool.

ELIZABETH. Then find the fool. Fast.

Blackout.

Scene Eleven
THE DUEL

An open space near Tyburn. LUCIUS, *now without* FROBISHER, *runs on. He stops, looks around, takes a deep breath, smiles. The dawn is breaking.* LUCIUS *sings.*

LUCIUS. And in the dawn as he walked home
With fal-de-ral-de-ratshit
He knew his time had surely come
With a hey hey nonny nonny –

He sees a figure coming towards him through the morning mist. This is the CAPTAIN.

God save you sir!

CAPTAIN. He will sir, he will. What a vile favoured wretch. What's your mystery, sir?

LUCIUS. Sir, I am a fool and there's an end to it.

CAPTAIN. Are you hurrying?

LUCIUS. I'm walking to Scotland.

CAPTAIN. Then you have time, you have time.

LUCIUS. For what?

CAPTAIN. Why, fool, for that thing which takes place on empty spaces in the half light of dawn.

LUCIUS. Swyving, sir?

CAPTAIN. No, clod. It is indeed a thing done in pairs, but it hath a sharper point.

LUCIUS. Not . . . duelling.

CAPTAIN. Yes duelling. I am second to one Master Gridling, a fearsome young blade, or so report has it out.

LUCIUS. You do not know the gentleman?

CAPTAIN. No indeed. I am, as it were, a connoisseur of the blade. I have fought some forty-three duels myself, seconded several score and have officiated at countless others. If there is to be a duel, word will come to me. And tonight the word 'Gridling' came to me as I sat in the shilling ordinary. Here, see my gear, I carry it everywhere.

The CAPTAIN *shows* LUCIUS *a large bag.*

Pistols, poignards, smelling salts, a measure – that's for distances – a handkerchief to drop to signal the start, maces – I love well a duel with maces, for your mace, wielded by a lusty fellow raises a fine and fatal welt – pray God it be maces tonight. Once – it was in the Low Country – I saw a Hollander contest the issue with a Portuguese: both armed with eight-foot axes, both men blindfold and set at forty paces. Lord, the horrid swishing of the blades as they beat around them in the dark! How the spectators skipp'd at their scythings. Two and a half hours were they lock'd in combat before they approach'd within earshot of one another, and all the time whirling their axes like windmills in a hurricano. At the finish, the Portuguese sliced the Dutchman's noddle at the neck, as clean as a butcher hacking off a foot of mutton for his dog. The head flew twenty feet in the air or else I am a Turk, and was caught at full stretch by a fishmonger's apprentice, and he, tucking it under his arm, makes off helter-skelter to his master's shop, with the mob in full pursuit, for they were polite fellows and did not relish the thought of their countryman's brains floating in the next day's bouillabasso.

LUCIUS. I see sir, you are indeed a lover of duels.

CAPTAIN. You have it, you have it! Give me a duel and let the rest of the world go hang on a mendicant's bellycord.

GRIDLING *comes on. He is dressed in the style of the Roarers with long shaggy locks and swollen eyes. He has a rusty rapier in his belt.*

GRIDLING. Are you the man they call the Captain?

CAPTAIN. Indeed. Master Gridling is it not?

GRIDLING. Indeed sir.

CAPTAIN. But what's that rapier, my worthy spadassino? Sure, it must have been dropped on a moor upon a damp St. Swithun's day and not recovered for a month. You do not intend to use that spike of rust tonight?

GRIDLING. Indeed no, good Captain –

CAPTAIN. Indeed no! That's the man. I have here a most rare pair of Moorish nose tongs, harmless enough at first nod, but Lord they can disfigure a man past recognition –

GRIDLING. Sir, I think you mistake –

CAPTAIN. Mistake? How mistake, sir?

GRIDLING. This is to be no mortal duel sir, fought with dagger, rapier or – saving your presence – Moorish nose tong.

CAPTAIN. Well, well, I am not averse to your pistol, your blunderbuss or musket. I have seen fellows fight i' the pitch dark with envenom'd glow-worms. I care not how 'tis done, so long as one falls down dead as a side of mutton at the close of the engagement.

GRIDLING. Sirrah, you mistake still. There will be none dead here this morning.

CAPTAIN. None dead! A duel and none dead!!!

GRIDLING. This is not to be a corporeal duel, sir, but, after the manner of the roarers, a duel of words.

CAPTAIN. Words?

GRIDLING. Aye sir, for so is the fashion in these enlightened times. When one, in the heat and passion of the ale house

abuses another, they do engage to see the matter to a finish
and seek satisfaction in insults traded at dawn.

CAPTAIN. Insults! This is the prologue and overture to a
quarrel, not the thing itself. You are, sir, as one who would
moisten a finger in his drab and think her soundly tupp'd.
Insults!

GRIDLING. Indeed, it is a modern notion, but I heard you
were a man game for anything and so would support me in
my righteous fight.

CAPTAIN. I? Second a man in a schoolyard battle of banter?
I have stood judgement while men hurled cannonballs at
each other as they do coconuts in an alley, and am I come to
this? What is my office as second, sir, to wipe the phlegm of
your adversary from your patchy cheeks?

GRIDLING. Here come the foe.

BEATRICE *and* ZANDA *come on. They are disguised as roaring
girls, fantastically dressed with spiked hair and painted, mask-like
faces.*

BEATRICE. He's here.

ZANDA. For his complexion alone he deserves to die.

BEATRICE. Good morrow, Master Gridling. So you go to it.

GRIDLING. I am yours, my roaring wench.

CAPTAIN. Sir, this is a woman.

BEATRICE. Wench me not, you trim-faced –

ZANDA. Save your insults, madam. Keep your powder dry for
the encounter.

BEATRICE. You commend me well.

CAPTAIN. They are both women.

GRIDLING. Sir, this is the new fashion. A woman may roar with
a man at no disadvantage.

CAPTAIN. A duel! You call me to a duel, my appetite is
whetted. And now I find you are gathered in the misty dawn
to trade profanities with a spike-haired moll.

GRIDLING. This is indeed the substance of the matter.

The CAPTAIN *falls on his knees.*

BEATRICE. This is the fool. How comes he here?

ZANDA. Through our good fortune. This makes our game. When our business is done, we convey him to your father and our credit grows.

BEATRICE. He'll recognise us.

ZANDA. Our disguise is perfect.

CAPTAIN. Oh world, oh wicked world! I have outlived my time. The youth is but degenerate and the noblest deeds have been performed already. Sir, on my honour I cannot stay.

GRIDLING. But I have no second.

CAPTAIN. This man is a clown by profession. I am a warrior. My hour is past, this gentleman's is here. He will be your second. I am for Smithfield. If my luck holds, I may yet see blood spilt in the early sunlight.

He goes. LUCIUS *coughs.*

GRIDLING. Well master . . .

LUCIUS. Bodkin, Lucius Bodkin.

GRIDLING. Can you stand this heavy office?

LUCIUS. I have stood for much, sir, I will surely stand for this.

ZANDA. Here comes judgement.

GRIDLING. Then towel me and fear the worst.

LUCIUS *wipes* GRIDLING'*s brow.* DRYSDALE, *an ancient scholar comes on. He carries huge tomes. He sets these down and perches on a stool.*

DRYSDALE. Masters. Mistresses. Are we well met?

GRIDLING. Indeed we are.

DRYSDALE. Then to the matter. What is the matter?

ZANDA. He called her a toe-rag. Last night. In the inn.

DRYSDALE. This is weighty matter, masters. And how do the gentlemen contend?

All look at LUCIUS.

LUCIUS. We contend . . . er . . . in these terms, your honour.

LUCIUS *clears his throat.*

Firstly it was a thing never said. Secondly, had it been said, it was surely another thing altogether and misheard. Thirdly that even allowing for its having been said in the first place and heard correctly in the second, it was but a pleasantry as one might call a bosom companion 'chuff' or 'shad' or 'arsehole'. Fourthly, that even given the fact that it was said aright, heard aright and construed aright, that the thing itself is a truth, namely that the auditor of the jibe stands before creation as the veriest toe-rag under the welkin. Your honour.

DRYSDALE. Faith, this man is but the second, we shall be here till Doomsday.

ZANDA. I'll knock the bastard's head off.

DRYSDALE. Let us make a start, masters. Fall to. Insult!!!

The combatants weave around. The seconds look on anxiously.

BEATRICE. Sheep-shagger!

GRIDLING. Curate's armpit!

BEATRICE. Nasal cavity!

GRIDLING. Undergarment!

BEATRICE. Toad-sucker!!

GRIDLING. Margery-prater!!!

ZANDA. Foul, this is canting talk.

DRYSDALE. Aye, but 'tis not yet seven of the morning. We may cant i' the hours of darkness, even though it be light.

ZANDA. Outrageous.

LUCIUS. Same for both sides.

ZANDA. Give him some cant then, girl.

The gloves are off. BEATRICE *winds herself up.*

BEATRICE. Traffic-niggling, strummel-libbing, cross-bitten simpler!!

GRIDLING *reels but comes back off the ropes.*

GRIDLING. Pullet-puller! Roger o' the buttery i' your shitten drawers.

BEATRICE. Grunting-cheat prat-mumbler!!! Dupping the bald

jigger of mooncalf nosegents with your greasen fambles!!!

GRIDLING *is on the back foot.*

GRIDLING. Pissing conduit! Looking glass! Thou bousy, bousy dell o' darkmans!!

BEATRICE. Snail-straddling pimple-pintled coxcomb-jockamed patrico panderer!! Gerry gan!! Bing a waste, wapper, bing a waste!!!!

GRIDLING. Er . . . goat-bucket.

This is clearly feeble. Even LUCIUS *looks disgusted.* ZANDA *appeals to* DRYSDALE.

ZANDA. Goat-bucket. What the pox is a goat-bucket?

LUCIUS. Clearly it's a bucket out of which a goat might feed.

ZANDA. Goats eat off the grass, they don't need crockery.

LUCIUS. Why then, a bucket into which a goat may shit.

ZANDA. They shit in the grass and all.

LUCIUS. Well then, it's . . . er . . .

DRYSDALE. It is a most wretched insult. For lo, does it not confuse Aquarius, the water carrier, the man with the bucket with Capricorn, the horned and bearded beast. 'Tis neither flesh nor fowl and a sure hit to the plaintiff.

ZANDA *and* BEATRICE *celebrate.*

LUCIUS. Get forward. Keep your weight evenly balanced. Watch her eyes. And don't stop dancing.

DRYSDALE. Come. To't again.

ZANDA. Have his knackers for breakfast.

DRYSDALE. To't I say, equivocate!

The COMBATANTS *come forward again, circling around one another.*

BEATRICE. 'Tis said, sir, by some old tosser, probably Plato, that we are all but a bunch of prats sat in a cave staring at reflections on the wall –

LUCIUS. Your worship, this is most unlettered.

DRYSDALE. I do concur most heartily, but since the thrust of

Plato's argument has been delivered, I must needs let it stand.

ZANDA. So shut it, dogsbreath.

BEATRICE. So how say you sir? Are you but a shadow on the wall, yea or nay?

GRIDLING. No, in good faith, for look how corporeal is my presence. Lay but a finger on me and you shall sense my physicality.

BEATRICE. Right.

BEATRICE *comes forward and nuts* GRIDLING *in the stomach. He goes down like a pile of pennies.*

BEATRICE. See. Nothing there. Didn't feel a thing.

LUCIUS. That must be a foul.

ZANDA. Nice one.

DRYSDALE. How say you, Master Gridling?

GRIDLING *writhes, unable to comment.*

LUCIUS. I say again, learned arbiter, this is most abject play.

ZANDA. Naff off, wankstain.

DRYSDALE *searches in a tome.*

DRYSDALE. 'Tis not a certain point, but yet, Master Zeno, the learned Greek did contend that an argument based on sense could be refuted on sense. Thus if the learned woman felt no sensation of the young man's stomach 'gainst her pate, then faith, *mutatis mutandis*, there was none, I give her the point.

The WOMEN *celebrate.*

LUCIUS. How now, Master Gridling, 'tis but two points gone.

GRIDLING *rises to his feet.*

GRIDLING. I do perceive I am made a fool of here. I am of the roaring persuasion. I am a man, if I may say, at the very summit point of fashion. I have three sets of outdoor boots and a canary that can sing in Greek. And yet I find I am mock'd, most roundly mock'd. I can rant and quarrel as lively as any man – or woman – between here and Barnet churchyard. And am I to be dandled in such terms by a pair of unread slatterns and a toothless pedant?

BEATRICE *draws a pistol from under her cloak and shoots him.*
GRIDLING *is briefly surprised and then, at some length, dead.*

BEATRICE. Well, master judge. How say you?

DRYSDALE. Ah . . . a most . . . ah . . . cogent and well-versed
argument which, it seems, the gentleman for all his fashion
and learning cannot refute.

ZANDA. Three-nil, total wipeout.

BEATRICE. I could not abide 'toothless', Master Drysdale. It
was an unpardonable slur on your surviving molar.

DRYSDALE. Quite so.

LUCIUS. You can't just . . .

Pause. All stare at LUCIUS.

LUCIUS. I mean you can't . . .

He gestures vaguely.

You can. You can. Yes I suppose there's no reason why not.
You can.

BEATRICE. We can indeed, Master Lucius.

LUCIUS. What?

BEATRICE *pays off* DRYSDALE *with some coins.*

BEATRICE. There's for your pains, Master Drysdale. We have
profited from your erudition.

DRYSDALE. And so have I, mistress. I'll to my study and
ponder Heraclitus.

DRYSDALE *takes the money and goes.*

LUCIUS *stares at the women. They stare back, removing their
make-up. He sees they are* BEATRICE *and* ZANDA.

ZANDA. If there be one pleasure unalloyed in all this wretched
life, I name it thus: the blessing of disguise.

BEATRICE. To be another. To wear the musks and fragrances
of someone else. To do another's murders. Fool?

LUCIUS. I was just on my way to Scotland.

BEATRICE. A mad, brave dash you made. You are something
short of Edgware.

LUCIUS. The Dutch. Your father set me up. He wanted me killed. Why?

BEATRICE. Don't take it personally.

ZANDA. I thought you were very funny.

LUCIUS. Really, did you think so?

Pause. The WOMEN *look at him.* LUCIUS *looks at* GRIDLING.

Who was he?

ZANDA. A small killing. Bravely done. You'll be tried for his murder. Probably in a week or so. That way we cover ourselves. Was it not most bravely done?

LUCIUS. Indeed. Most bravely.

ZANDA *puts an iron collar round* LUCIUS*'s neck. The collar is fastened to two chains.* BEATRICE *and* ZANDA *take a chain each.*

ZANDA. Back to London?

BEATRICE. Back to London.

They lead LUCIUS *off.*

Some moments, then the sound of someone approaching at a breathless, wheezing run. It is the CAPTAIN. *He stands and stares at the body, exhausted by his dash.*

CAPTAIN. Pox, I have missed it!!!!

Blackout.

Scene Twelve
THE PRISONER

WARBURTON. My game is made. All but made. And that 'all but' sticks in my throat. Davenport and the mob rise and fall and he now stares outwards from the Clink, polishing the iron bars with his eyebrows. The Bishop for his suspect sermon entertains himself in the same dungeon. These seeming extremists are cast down, Frobisher, the middle man, is dead, and I should have his place but for this fool. Because there is no corpse, and no proved criminal, Her Majesty holds me much at fault. If my guards cannot find him I am Wednesday's mutton.

A noise outside.

Who's there?

BEATRICE *and* ZANDA *come in at the run. They hurl* LUCIUS *onto the floor in front of* WARBURTON.

ZANDA. What price this prize, my master!

WARBURTON *reaches down, lifts up* LUCIUS*'s face, then hurls him down again.*

WARBURTON. The fool! My girls, have you done this?

He embraces them.

ZANDA. We were out shooting rabbits in the dawn, and arrowed down this buck.

WARBURTON. My giddy girls, my huntresses, my pair of chaste Dianas! You, sweet fool, will straightway to the Queen where she will deem such punishment as she thinks fit.

LUCIUS. I did what you told me.

WARBURTON. Abduct a body?

LUCIUS. A few bad jokes, that's all my crime. You set me up.

WARBURTON. Politics. Laughter. We live in dangerous worlds.

He takes LUCIUS *by the chain and makes to go.*

You, Zanda, this ensures your freedom.

He goes, dragging LUCIUS. BEATRICE *shouts after him.*

BEATRICE. And mine?

ZANDA. You have won your freedom through your own bold deed.

BEATRICE. And now?

ZANDA. Now prayer and devotion. We must play the innocents.

BEATRICE. My blood is up, I cannot fust i' the chapel.

ZANDA. But you must. The murder is completed. Dissembling well still lies before you.

BEATRICE. I would go forth tonight again in strange apparel and taste mad drink, tobacco and brave boys.

ZANDA. No. Your father calls us chaste Dianas. So must we seem when Gridling's death is posted.

BEATRICE. Give me some drug, then, to cool my killing fever.

ZANDA. Think only what you owe yourself and me.

BEATRICE. What I owe you? What's that?

ZANDA. I have freed you from a rusty marriage, but still am in my chains. Your father talks of my freedom but that means nothing unless he grants me other favours. He promised me a lady's life if I push'd on his plot. You must pursue him with my suit.

BEATRICE. All in good time.

ZANDA. All in good time I dragged you off the hook of wedlock. Now shift yourself to help my cause.

BEATRICE. Shift yourself, maidservant, to bring tobacco when I call for it.

ZANDA. There is narcotic enough for you in your neglected prayer book. Fetch it for yourself.

ZANDA goes. BEATRICE takes out the pistol. Looks at it.

Blackout.

Scene Thirteen
THE PERFORMANCE

ELIZABETH *on her throne in a spotlight.*

ELIZABETH. There have been some who thought, in our reported illness, to further their own ends through conspiracy and intrigue. But where malefactors be, so be there hearts where good report abounds. And though we grieve for our lamented Frobisher, yet we rejoice that in this hour of crisis, when so many played the jackal part, that Richard Warburton should have proved a lion.

WARBURTON *appears in a spotlight on the other side of the stage.*

Accordingly we elevate him to our dear Frobisher's place and name him our chiefest privy councillor.

WARBURTON *kneels. An ABRAHAM MAN appears, jangling a*

chain of state office. He places the chain around
WARBURTON's *neck then holds up a mirror. Another*
ABRAHAM MAN *arrives with a mace and hands it to*
WARBURTON. WARBURTON *admires himself for a moment,
then dismisses the* ABRAHAM MEN *with a nod. He stands in an
attitude of triumph, waving the mace aloft. His spotlight goes out.*

More light comes up around ELIZABETH. LUCIUS *is prostrate at
her feet.*

ELIZABETH. Lucius Bodkin.

Pause.

Get up.

Pause.

Get up!

LUCIUS *slowly gets into a kneeling position.*

I've seen enough hairlines. Get up. Bald patches, dandruff
harvests, lice farms. Get up. On your feet. Say something.

LUCIUS. I . . . your highness. I beseech you to –

ELIZABETH. Not that. You know what I want to hear. Make me
laugh.

LUCIUS. Laugh?

ELIZABETH. That is your mystery.

LUCIUS. Yes.

ELIZABETH. Then to't. You are no courtier, scraping the
ground with your nose. To your mystery and make me laugh.

Pause.

LUCIUS. Yes. Er. There was this Spaniard. With the . . .

ELIZABETH. Three foot ruff, yes, don't you have any new
material?

LUCIUS. The new material is . . . well . . . it's new and . . .

ELIZABETH. Yes?

ELIZABETH. You wouldn't like it.

ELIZABETH. Why not?

LUCIUS. It's too . . .

ELIZABETH. Too what?

LUCIUS. It's about you.

ELIZABETH. I'm glad people still think about me. It's very flattering. We'll have this new material now. Play.

LUCIUS. There's nothing to laugh about.

ELIZABETH. What do you mean, nothing to laugh about?

LUCIUS. I'm set up. I have to run for my life. I make it clear of London. And the bastards still get me. I'm up in front of you, I know I'm for the chop. So I don't feel particularly funny.

ELIZABETH. I don't think you understand. I'm not asking *you* to laugh. I'm asking you to make *me* laugh.

LUCIUS. I don't feel like it.

ELIZABETH. I saw your father once.

Pause.

One Accession Day. After the feast. He had us in fits. Him and his hawk. I allowed him to kiss my hand afterwards. I asked him if he was always so merry. He said he wasn't merry at all, he had come that afternoon from burying his wife. I wondered at this and he said: 'It is my mystery. When you need to be merry, I must make you so, whether I am merry myself or not.' He was right. I have after all, stuck to *my* mystery. I have stuck to it for forty-five years. I can't say 'I don't feel like being Queen.' Now make me laugh.

LUCIUS. You're going to execute me tomorrow.

ELIZABETH. We'll make a bargain. As things stand you are condemned to die by hanging, drawing and quartering. The more you make me laugh, the more I'll reduce your sentence. So a couple of guffaws'll get it down to plain hanging, a real belly-laugh and you'll earn yourself a nice straightforward beheading.

LUCIUS. What do you want me to be funny about?

ELIZABETH. I'm trying to die. I've been trying to die for weeks now. You haven't got any jokes about that have you? It might help.

LUCIUS. Dying is a difficult subject.

ELIZABETH. I spent so much of my reign hanging on to life.

For the good of the nation. Religion. Smallpox. There seemed to be so many ways of tripping over into my grave. Now I can't shake the habit. I need to die for the good of the nation. And I can't do it.

LUCIUS. We could swap places tomorrow, that would crack it for you.

ELIZABETH. Monarchs are not executed in this country.

LUCIUS. Well, executions are the only sort of death I've had on my mind lately.

ELIZABETH. I suppose I'll have to lump it, then. Be funny about executions.

LUCIUS. All right. All right. Executions? Don't talk to me about executions. I've seen more executions than you've had hot . . . no probably not. It's necessary, you see, I know it's necessary. I like a good burning, myself. Amazing how much heat one man can generate, specially if he's a Bishop, pure tallow your average Bishop, awful lot of candlepower in a Bishop, very welcome of a winter's day. I like to get there early, right at the front, stick a few chestnuts under the faggots, programme, get your official programme. Your Bishop though does tend to spoil it with the speeches and all, chuntering away in Latin when you're waiting for the action: 'Hodie sum barbecue. Sed sum barbecue Dei.' 'Get on with it, we haven't got all day.' 'You've got all day', says his Grace, 'It's me that won't be around for lunch.' 'Less rabbit, mitre-features. Chop up his crozier for kindling, let's have a decent blaze.'

Then there's hanging, drawing and quartering. Did you see Will Parry die? I did, I was a boy. Condemned for high treason. Against your good self as I recall. The executioner was Ralph Crispin. Hanging, drawing and quartering. Sounds cushy doesn't it, till you realise what's involved. The hanging was the easy bit, he just swung around up there, fighting for breath admittedly, but still swinging, swinging till they cut him down. Funny the way it gave him a hard-on, four thousand of us there, we didn't know where to look. But he's a card, Will, he shouts out: 'Is my wife in the crowd?' 'No, Will.' 'Oh well then, anybody?' But Crispin won't have any of it. The privy parts are to be cut off, it's on his list, it's necessary, so the chopper comes down on Will's chopper. Will knows it's necessary, I know it's necessary, but the waste and the blood. Then we get to the drawing, now that's something else. A couple of quick incisions and then Crispin shoves the old hand right in there, scrabbles around a bit and finally comes up with all this offal, bits of gut and liver and yesterday's breakfast. Slaps the lot down on this dinky little pewter dish, nice pile of butcher's best and sets fire to the lot while Will is standing there watching. I thought they might offer him a bit of mustard on the side and make him eat it, but no, we know the limits, we're not some bunch of Dagos are we, this is London, and it's not necessary, some of it's necessary, but not eating your own guts.

We pass on smoothly to the quartering. Quartering? I always feel sorry for the horses, roped up to this gutless, prickless corpse, sorry not corpse, he's still alive is Will, but the horses are pulling away, these clapped out old shire horses, straining away and still there's some bits of sinew and gristle which are holding this man together, they have to whip the horses, get them to pull harder but it's necessary I know it's English and necessary, four horses, one in each corner straining away, sweat on their flanks and eventually something snaps, but he's still alive, some joint gives way, a bit of leg on a rope, the horse runs clear, dragging the stump into the crowd, and then an arm and I know it's necessary, even though he is still alive and they throw water on his face to stop him fainting, and I'm only nine years old at the front, I'm learning that it's necessary because of our English restraint, and then another leg, there's not a lot left of Will Parry, but he's plucky, he's English, he's still alive, we can take it guv, only the last horse is some clapped out nag, hasn't the strength to wrench the poxy arm out of its socket. The crowd start booing, we don't want this, we want a nice clean job, we are English after all and we know it's necessary, we want a nice clean torso with the guts out and the knackers chopped off, and we're having to make do with this arm still hanging off him, but we're tolerant, we can tolerate it, so they sit him up and he shouts out, and this is the best bit, he shouts out 'God Save the Queen', 'cos he knows it's necessary too, he's a stringy torso pumping blood and there's only one thing in the world he wants, he wants the Almighty to save *you*, wants the Almighty to save *you*, wants the Almighty to save *you* who's signed the order for all this to happen, but we know it's necessary because we're English, but now he's said that, we don't want him to say anything else, look bad if he changed his mind, so it's out with his tongue, wrench with a big pair of pincers like a tooth being drawn, surprisingly long a tongue once you've got it all out, the gaffer waves it around and we all cheer, 'cos it's the tongue that just said 'God Save the Queen', but Will Parry, he doesn't look so chipper, even though he has kept an arm, still, Ralph Crispin sees to that, it's on the list, it has to be done, swish, chop, easy as blinking the arm's off, it jumps three yards but Will is still hanging in there, you never know, the Queen might come up with a reprieve at the last minute, but no, nothing, good old Ralph knows it's time, he's had years of practice and slowly, so slowly, he looks down at Will and raises the axe and chops him at the neck and the head rolls and the whole . . . thing twitches and shudders and we all . . . just stand there. Because it's over now. There's nothing more we can think of doing to him. Some people shuffle off. But I stay. As they get all the bits together. Pile them up. And Ralph Crispin says, about the bits, that they'll be disposed of at Her Majesty's pleasure. And more people start to go, but there's something I haven't understood. The guards start clearing the crowd away, 'Ain't you got hovels to go to, arf, arf, come on sonny, naff off', and I say: 'What does it mean?' 'What does what mean?' 'What does it mean, Her Majesty's pleasure?' And the guard points at Will Parry, bundled up on a sort of stretcher and he says 'That is, son. That is Her Majesty's pleasure.' And I thought, yes, it is necessary, I know it's necessary. It is necessary isn't it?

ELIZABETH. You have not made me laugh.

LUCIUS. Why then, perhaps this is not altogether fool.

Pause.

ELIZABETH. There's an Englishman, a Dutchman and a Frenchman, all sitting in a tavern discussing politics. The Englishman says: 'We don't mind about politics as long as we have a monarch who runs the country.' The Dutchman says: 'We don't mind who runs the country as long as it's not a monarch.' And the Frenchman says: 'We don't mind who the monarch is as long as he doesn't run the country.'

LUCIUS *laughs a little.*

LUCIUS. Not bad. Not bad.

ELIZABETH. We are at war with ourselves. God wills it so. We cannot make the light all ours. We are ignorants in a world of shades. I choose to limit the war. A Catholic burnt here, a Puritan with severed thumbs out there. These are but pinpricks in a world of blood. In Europe they pile up their dead in thousands on account of civil wars. We are more civilised. Make the common populace know fear and they will tread a narrow path. There has been one overriding virtue in my reign – its length. Nearly fifty years where no one asks: 'Who leads us?' Take away that question and the sum of misery dwindles. It doesn't matter who is the leader, only that the question is not asked. People are happy when their eyes are on the ploughshare in the furrow, not when they send envious glances to the stars. You did not make me laugh.

LUCIUS. I'm sorry, I keep thinking about what's going to happen to me.

ELIZABETH. You're innocent, I know.

LUCIUS. I was set up to slag off those Dutch geezers and then – what?

ELIZABETH. Of course you're innocent. You were a pawn in a power struggle.

LUCIUS. Why don't you let me go then?

Pause.

ELIZABETH. If you're a woman in power you have two choices. Either surround yourself with stupid men and trample all over them. Or surround yourself with clever men who will compete against each other. The first way produces bad government. You think you're right about everything, because no one dares to contradict you. So I chose the other way. I chose clever men. Plenty of ideas, plenty of arguments. You doubt your own wisdom every day and that keeps you on the true path. The only problem is that the men around you will fight each other. The cunning will win. Warburton wins. I could execute him tomorrow. But there would be no one to run the country when I'm gone. So. It's you tomorrow instead. If I don't punish you, people won't believe Warburton's story. And then we'd have no government which is the worst government of all.

LUCIUS. That's wrong.

ELIZABETH. It's good for the country.

LUCIUS. It doesn't make me feel better.

ELIZABETH. No. I see that. Only it's necessary. Understand?

LUCIUS. These things should not be necessary. Whatever end they seek to justify is wrong. Why do we move so slowly towards a saner commonwealth? I think it's because we do not intend to move that way at all. Our seeming progress is only incidental, undone tomorrow in a trice. Our aim is only for the dark, and you are the one that leads us to the pit. This Queen we shall cast down.

ELIZABETH. What was that?

LUCIUS. I don't know. Just a line going through my head. 'This Queen we shall cast down.' Might make a rant out of it.

ELIZABETH. 'This Queen we shall cast down.' It has a ring. You can work on it in The Clink tonight.

LUCIUS. Could do it as my last words. Good to go out on a show.

ELIZABETH. It would be good to go out at all. I'll think of you tonight. You have made me melancholy, fool. Will that help me to die?

LUCIUS. I hope so.

ELIZABETH. Your father was funnier, but then, I was younger. Take him away.

HIERONYMOUS *comes on with the hawk on his shoulder. He carries a lantern. It's suddenly very dark, with only the light from the lantern and a spotlight on* ELIZABETH *remaining.* ELIZABETH *scratches with a pen on some paper.*

The sentence on the fool Lucius Bodkin is . . . the sentence on the fool is . . . the sentence is . . . .

HIERONYMOUS. Come on, son. This way.

Blackout.

Scene Fourteen
THE EXECUTION

A cell in The Clink prison. THE BISHOP *and* DAVENPORT *stare at each other. Both are festooned with chains.*

THE BISHOP. I don't care what happens, but I do want a cell on my own before they top me.

DAVENPORT. It's a *prison*. It's not meant to be nice –

THE BISHOP. I know what it is, I own the poxy thing.

DAVENPORT. Then you should know –

THE BISHOP. *And* I wish I wasn't sharing it with some venereal left-footer, *and* I wish there was some clean straw, *and* I wish the bloody door would open so we could get out.

The door opens. A hand propels LUCIUS *into the cell. The door shuts again.*

I do wish I hadn't said that last bit. I really do repent all that about the door. Who in Christ's bowels are you?

LUCIUS. I used to be a fool, now I'm sort of an all-round entertainer.

THE BISHOP. Oh yeah, and I'm Bishop of Winchester.

LUCIUS. I've played in front of royalty, mate.

THE BISHOP. Haven't we all, sonny.

LUCIUS. What's going to happen to us?

THE BISHOP. Him and me, being of the nobility will be looking forward to a nice quick clean beheading. You, being a low-born sort of slag will doubtless face something slower and wittier like being mumbled to death by terrapins.

DAVENPORT. I am a Catholic nobleman, the Pope is even now preparing diplomatic moves to save me. I am confident that –

The door opens again.

A GAOLER. All right. All you lot. Outside.

THE BISHOP (*to* DAVENPORT). Any more bright ideas, dogsbreath?

Drums. The three prisoners march to a position at the front of the stage. During this, lights pick out ELIZABETH, *remote from the action on her throne.*

ELIZABETH. We princes are set on stages in the sight and view of all the world duly observed: the eyes of many behold our actions: a spot is soon spied in our garments: a blemish quickly noted in our doings.

DAVENPORT, LUCIUS *and* THE BISHOP *line up facing front.*

A spotlight picks out ELIZABETH *on the throne.*

ELIZABETH. Know that in conspiring to overthrow the crown you have offended mightily against your sovereign and your God. The penalties against you are severe, but cannot hope to match your crimes. Edmund, Bishop of Winchester.

THE BISHOP *steps forward and kneels, putting his hands and head on the block. The lights concentrate on the faces of* ELIZABETH *and* THE BISHOP.

Seditious mountebank, what say you?

THE BISHOP. God save the Queen!

A scything sound from the violin, drums, a rattling of chains. THE BISHOP *'s light goes out.*

ELIZABETH. Sir Richard Davenport.

DAVENPORT *steps forward and kneels, repeating the movements of* THE BISHOP. *Again the lights concentrate so we see only* DAVENPORT *'s and* ELIZABETH *'s faces.*

Treasonable dog, what say you?

DAVENPORT. God save the Queen!

Again the scything from the violin, drums, the rattling of chains. DAVENPORT *'s light goes out.*

ELIZABETH. Lucius Bodkin, fool.

LUCIUS *follows the same movements as* DAVENPORT *and* THE BISHOP.

Prattling conspirator, what say you?

LUCIUS *opens his mouth but nothing comes out.*

What say you?

Silence again.

What say you?

Lights concentrate on LUCIUS *'s open, silent mouth. Chains, drums, violin. Suddenly silence.*

Blackout.

Scene Fifteen
THE WOUNDED MAN

In the darkness, a knocking noise, like a bone tapping against a skull.

Lights up on BUTLER*'s shop. He is operating a small printing press. This is indicated by a battered old typewriter and a duplicating machine with a drum and a handle. The knocking noise has become a hammering on the door.* BUTLER *reacts nervously, trying to hide the printed pages.*

BUTLER. Oh Jesus!!

The hammering increases. BUTLER *rushes to and fro frantically.*

Christ! I'm coming. Christ!!

The door is battered down. BUTLER *draws a dagger.* LUCIUS *comes in. His right hand has been chopped off. He is bleeding profusely.* BUTLER *drops the dagger.*

LUCIUS. God save the Queen!

BUTLER. Amen to that.

LUCIUS. God save the Queen I say!

BUTLER. I say amen.

LUCIUS *advances on the machine, picks up a page, reads.*

LUCIUS. God save the Queen, but what's this, 'On the advantages to the populace of insurrection in the Commonwealth.' This is not 'God save the Queen', this is sedition.

BUTLER. What do you want? (*Noticing the wound.*) Jesus, what have they done to you?

LUCIUS. You have a printing press, you have the power of the word. God save the Queen. I want you.

BUTLER. What?

LUCIUS. I have a speech that will inflame the mob, God save the Queen and you shall print it!

LUCIUS *falls in a faint.* BUTLER *stares.*

Blackout.

Scene Sixteen
THE MURDERER

BEATRICE *alone.*

BEATRICE. I see his face. A piece of parchment scratched on by a child and left out in the rain. The mud of London's fields spattering his eyes and nose. Mud on my boots. After killing, every action so loud. I tug at a broken nail, the rip of it deafens me. Again and again I feel the jolt of the pistol in my hand. The ease of it. The ecstasy. How now?

ZANDA *is there.*

ZANDA. My lady. Will you come to bed? It is time.

BEATRICE. For bed, no, surely. It is night and time to throw on our roaring apparel and out into the darkness.

ZANDA. We will act the perfect maid and lady and follow daily customs. Your father must harbour no suspicion against us. I will brush your hair and soothe you, then you'll sleep.

BEATRICE. My hair is mud and gunpowder. You will not brush it out, I like it so.

ZANDA. Tomorrow we will fetch water to wash it. Now sit.

BEATRICE. Who gives the orders here?

ZANDA. You are the mistress in the house, but I am Queen in the streets and we have brought the street stink here into your chambers. You do not know what musks and mists can cover murder but I do and you will swallow my prescription. Now sit.

BEATRICE *sits on the floor, but not where* ZANDA *has indicated.* ZANDA *goes to her and brushes.*

When I was a slave to the Spaniards, I was their thing to use as they wished. I fetched for them, skivvied. They took me, sleeping, in sickness, they didn't care. One was the ship's doctor. He grabbed me, sudden while I slept upon the deck. I turned and fisted him, he fell, heavy, his head striking a cannon. Dead. I held his body up and nailed it to the mast. The crew looked on. They never troubled me again. I said: 'Now I am your doctor.' I had broken the chain.

BEATRICE. The chain.

ZANDA. As you have broken yours.

BEATRICE. And what should I do now?

ZANDA. Why, anything, you have freed yourself.

BEATRICE. Until the next suitor. Do I kill him too?

ZANDA. You wait. You live from day to day. You relish the snapping of your chain.

BEATRICE. There is a chain. It links the dumb stones to God. That is what they taught me. For look, the lodestone is above all stones for it seems, in its iron attraction to have some life and so is somewhat of a plant, fibrous, reaching out beyond itself. And some plants of the sea, in their sucking and pulsating imitate the life of creatures. The ape walks upright, the ape apes the man and men, some saintly men are close to angels who fly all the way to God. This is the chain, this is the living chain and I have snapped it.

ZANDA. I meant the chain that bound you to your father.

BEATRICE. That is not the chain!

BEATRICE *stands suddenly. The hairbrush drops to the floor.*

I have snapped a link in the chain of being, a small snip to a link and now the chain is sundered, and what is outside the chain? They told me hell, and they told me falsely. I killed but I am not in the furnace. I am in the thrilling region, the realm of ice where the air is dizzy.

ZANDA. My lady, I have a soothing plant that you may smoke to calm you –

BEATRICE. I have their secret! I know the secret the men have, that they carry with them, which gives them power! The swords on their hips, their furtive pistols. Killing is exciting, it is power. You knew that from your slave days and yet you kept it from me.

ZANDA. I was in desperate straits.

BEATRICE. And so was I, and now I am delivered. I am no longer one who waits, looks on and nods agreement. I change the face of the earth. I squeeze a trigger and the world is changed. There is nothing I cannot do!

ZANDA. You still have everything to do. You must not trumpet out this murder. Your father will be high in anger at this death and you must play bereavement to the hilt.

BEATRICE. I have done with playing. From now I shall play myself at all times.

ZANDA. The Queen grows sicker. This is the report from every stair and corridor. When she is dead, your power in the court is gone. All you can ever be is a drain on your father's exchequer or a quim for trading on the market. You have 'scaped one husband, you cannot 'scape them all.

BEATRICE. This is not so. I am a killer. I am one of them.

ZANDA *seizes* BEATRICE.

ZANDA. You and I have been as sisters! We have brought the two halves of the globe together and made a safe cocoon to live in, an egg where we have dwelt in safety from the world of men. The shell is shattered now. We must stand together. Without me you will have no access to the world of pleasure and die a country death with a fat husband. Without you I have no privilege and cannot be protected from the curs who call me blackamoor and spit upon my skin.

BEATRICE. And still you do not see it. They put a prayer book in my hand and told me God would see my every sin. But I have done the worst, the final sin and am not seen. I have not put myself in prison, I have burst out. You talk of freedom here on earth, freedom of the body, when I speak of my eternal soul.

ZANDA. You must conceal this murder. If you broadcast it abroad, my complicity will be much blamed.

BEATRICE. It was a noble thought and you must own it.

ZANDA. Speak lower! Your guilt, once known will be laden at my door.

WARBURTON *comes in. He wears the chain of office.*

WARBURTON. Why what's here? The servant handling the mistress?

BEATRICE. Thoughts of death and living, nothing else.

ZANDA. My lady has a fever. She should lie down and –

BEATRICE. Why father, you have gained the chain of office –

WARBURTON. There is other news. Foul deeds. The man who was to have been her husband –

BEATRICE. Shot. Through the heart. Silver bullets. In the mud beyond Edgware.

WARBURTON. My news has raced before me –

BEATRICE. I have the pistol here. And here the murderer's hand.

Pause.

ZANDA. This is her raving, it signifies nothing –

BEATRICE. Father, I have not thanked you for my education.

ZANDA. My Lady Beatrice, you shall go straight to bed –

BEATRICE. Not for the Latin and Greek whipped into me, but for your education in the art of politic murder. For did you not show me the way with friend Frobisher, did you not send the Bishop and Lord Davenport to the axe. But there is a fault I find in my killing education, that I must go to finishing school at the feet of our slave. You taught me only the grammar and syntax of murder, but Zanda rendered me the gift of tongues –

ZANDA. This is all lies and fancy –

BEATRICE. – she put the pistol in my hand and gave me the trigger lesson. I shot the man you wanted for my husband and now I stand forever free.

WARBURTON. Zanda, fetch instantly two men of the household to bind my daughter down, she cannot be let loose abroad –

BEATRICE. I am let loose for ever.

She threatens them with the pistol.

I cannot be confined within my prayer book room. I am now out among the world. There is no chain you can devise that will ever drag me back. I was never innocent. I watched the worms eating at the stair and, in my secret thoughts, considered them good. But now I take a hatchet to the banisters and smile. I will leave my hairbrush.

BEATRICE *goes.* WARBURTON *makes to follow.*

ZANDA. Leave her. She is unhinged.

WARBURTON. You have done this.

ZANDA. Why me? We have conspired, the three of us together for our several profits –

WARBURTON. But I took care. The part she bore was light with no contagion in it –

ZANDA. You are the contagion. You have swooped on power like a clumsy eagle and your own eggs are shattered –

WARBURTON. But I have the power. The Queen this day conferred on me the ministry that shall look forward to the reign of James. I will bestride the worlds of yesterday and tomorrow. I am the bridge between two sovereigns –

ZANDA. To be blown up by some cunning sapper –

WARBURTON. You shall not cross me –

ZANDA. Then do not lay your daughter's crimes with me. She is your flesh. Now, to our business.

WARBURTON. Business?

ZANDA. I undertook the manufacture of certain crimes to speed you on to power. These I effected and now you wear the chain. I had my price and now I want it paid. Where is my freedom?

WARBURTON. We will speak anon, now is not the time. I must retrieve my daughter.

ZANDA. Give me but power, you said, and I would name my price. This debt is not so easily forgot.

WARBURTON. It is not forgot. It is but postponed.

ZANDA. Postponed till when? Your mighty office will fit you out with many an excuse to thrust my claims away –

WARBURTON. You are my slave! I paid gold coin in the market place. I throw away the key at my own leisure.

ZANDA. This leisure may prove costly.

WARBURTON. You cannot threaten me. The Queen has posted statutes forbidding Blackamoors the realm. You remain in England only at my protection. Think on that. Now to my daughter. If your hand shows any stains of guilt in that business, you may fear the worst.

WARBURTON *goes.* ZANDA *stands a moment. Then picks up the hairbrush. She brushes her hair.*

Blackout.

Scene Seventeen
THE PAMPHLET

BUTLER's *shop.* LUCIUS *sits with pen and ink, composing.*
BUTLER *is at the typewriter 'typesetting' what he's writing. They've*
nearly finished.

LUCIUS. Having a stump makes you interesting you know. It
   gets people talking.

BUTLER. Are you writing this bleeding rant or what?

LUCIUS. Sorry, John.

BUTLER. A stump is a stump, right.

LUCIUS. It's still a novelty to me.

BUTLER. You're lucky it's not a neck stump. She must have
   taken a fancy to you.

LUCIUS. She did not take a fancy to me. All right.

BUTLER. All right.

LUCIUS. I was innocent. She knew. And she still chopped me.

BUTLER. All right. Now will you shift it, I've got a bastard
   radical puritan pamphlet to do after this. You're not the only
   dissenter in London who wants printing.

LUCIUS. Great medium, though. Beats all that flogging round
   the circuit. You do it once, it's there for ever.

BUTLER. Till they seize them and burn them.

LUCIUS. Yeah?

BUTLER. Yeah. And the printing presses. And the blokes who
   print them.

LUCIUS. Another dangerous game.

BUTLER. Aren't they all?

LUCIUS. Right, the last line: 'And rule ourselves the better.'

BUTLER. 'And rule ourselves the better.' That's what I've got.
   We had that half an hour ago.

LUCIUS. Print it. That's it. It's simple. The language of the
   streets. Direct. Pithy.

BUTLER. You're the governor.

During the following, BUTLER *takes the stencil out of the typewriter and winds it onto the drum of the duplicator.*

LUCIUS. All that Alchemical stuff. Is there no call for that?

BUTLER. There are cycles. Cycles of need and cycles of belief. Like cogs. They mesh with each other in different places at different times. Sometimes people believe in things they don't need. Like now. Sometimes people don't believe in what they do need. People don't believe in sorcery any more, all that stuff my Dad taught me. But it's still there. When they need it, they'll come back to me. And I'll still have it, get me? It'll come back. Meanwhile, move with the times. Learn the new technology.

BUTLER *turns the handle. Pages cascade onto the floor.* LUCIUS *picks one up.*

LUCIUS. The beauty of print. Clean characters stamped on a page. No more standing in the firing line. No more pissing in the wind. From now on, it's there in black and white for ever.

LUCIUS *picks up a bundle of the completed rants. He runs, scattering them around the stage for the* ABRAHAM MEN *to pick up.*

LUCIUS. LON-DON!!! LON-DON!!! LON-DON!!! LON-DON!!!

He runs off shouting. The ABRAHAM MEN *appear for the next scene.*

Scene Eighteen
THE RANT

The ABRAHAM MEN *assemble from various directions. Each has a copy of* LUCIUS's *rant. One or two of them pick copies from off the walls of the set. There are various attempts to make it out, but none of them can read.*

ABRAHAM 1. What is it, plague words?

ABRAHAM 2. No. You get a picture with plague.

ABRAHAM 3. Skull.

ABRAHAM 2. Skull, yeah. Plague words. Skull picture.

ABRAHAM 3. Bones.

ABRAHAM 2. Bones, yeah.

ABRAHAM 1. Could scran it.

ABRAHAM 2. Cramp-wit.

ABRAHAM 3. Bung-brain.

ABRAHAM 1 (*eating it*). Not bad.

ABRAHAM 2. Oh bene peck, bene peck.

ABRAHAM 3. Yonder. Mort.

BEATRICE *has come on. She's pale and ragged. The* ABRAHAM
MEN *look her over. They crowd round, curious, not threatening.*

ABRAHAM 1. Come up from the country have we?

BEATRICE. No.

ABRAHAM 2. Town voice, town mort.

ABRAHAM 3. Gentry mort.

Pause. They look at her and touch her clothes. The THIRD
ABRAHAM MAN *hands her a pamphlet.*

ABRAHAM 1. Scran? Peck?

BEATRICE *looks at it. Starts to read it.*

ABRAHAM 3. Schooled mort, reading mort.

The SECOND ABRAHAM MAN *points at the pamphlet, then at*
BEATRICE*'s mouth.*

BEATRICE. Read it? You want me to read it?

ABRAHAM 2. Song. The man with the stump. A song.

ABRAHAM 1. I had a song once.

ABRAHAM 3. Shhssht. Hearken.

BEATRICE *reads.*

ABRAHAM 2. Aloud, like.

BEATRICE. 'The mob through all the ages' –

ABRAHAM 1. That's us.

ABRAHAM 3. Hearken!

BEATRICE. 'The mob through all the ages
　　Have loved the Prince and Priest
　　Who latch us in our cages –'

Tableau. BEATRICE *reading to the* ABRAHAM MEN.

On the other side of the stage, a spotlight picks out ELIZABETH.
She is pale and very weak.

ELIZABETH. I have lain down across a chasm and made a
　　bridge of my body so that my people could walk from
　　darkness into light. I have been the Virgin Queen to all my
　　knights. And yet, at the end, it is I who will set a taper to the
　　round table. I have buried a world of chivalry and brought,
　　squealing into life, a world of gold. All for the love of my
　　people.

She is still in her pool of light. The ABRAHAM MEN *are restless,*
angry, slowly coming together around BEATRICE. LUCIUS
appears on the other side of the stage. He watches.

The ABRAHAM MEN *and* BEATRICE *perform* LUCIUS*'s rant.*
At first they are tentative, then they gain confidence until they begin
to march as a body. They turn towards ELIZABETH, *ranting and*
marching until they are surrounding her.

THE RANT OF THE ABRAHAMS

ABRAHAM MEN. The mob through all the ages
　　Have loved the Prince and Priest
　　Who latch us in our cages
　　And give us of the least.

　　With a hone a hone a hone
　　Our cramp rings we unfetter
　　This Queen we shall cast down
　　And rule ourselves the better.

　　To you whose pride has pained us
　　We vent our canting song
　　This reign that hath enchained us
　　Shall not endure for long

　　With a hone a hone a hone
　　Our cramp rings we unfetter
　　This Queen we shall cast down
　　And rule ourselves the better.

　　From us you milled our riches
　　To you we foolish gave

We rankest filching ruffians
Shall thrust you in your grave

With a hone a hone a hone
Our cramp rings we unfetter
This Queen we shall cast down
And rule ourselves the better.

The ABRAHAM MEN *are swarming around the base of*
ELIZABETH*'s throne, threatening insurrection. One of them is*
held up on the shoulders of the others. He tries to pull ELIZABETH
down.

Suddenly, ELIZABETH *stands for the first time in the play. She*
rants back at the ABRAHAM MEN.

ELIZABETH. Plague dogs
    Gutter curs
    Ditch-swilling bitches
    Sweat-swervers
    Swaddlers
    Cat-prigging witches
    Freshwater mariners
    Baskets with itches
    Maggot men
    Clapper crabs
    Filch all, thieve all
    Farcers
    Foisterers
    Suckers of the weevil
    Shag-eared sleazy slobs
    Fambling your scrawny knobs
    Dup well your greasy gobs
    Drink the Queen's Evil!

ELIZABETH *spits repeatedly on the* ABRAHAM MEN.
Immediately, they run for cover, huddling into the remotest parts of
the stage, protecting their heads and faces with their hands.
BEATRICE *stands her ground for a moment, then runs to the side*
of the stage.

When all the ABRAHAM MEN *are cowering,* ELIZABETH
resumes her throne.

ELIZABETH. Though God has raised me high, yet this I count
    the glory of my crown, that I have reigned with your loves. It
    is not my desire to live or reign longer than my life and reign
    shall be for your good. And though you have had, and may

have, many mightier and wiser princes sitting in this seat, yet
you never had, nor shall have, any that will love you better.

The ABRAHAM MEN *are stunned. Their mood is utterly
transformed. Slowly they begin to hum, then change the words of*
LUCIUS's *rant into a madrigal of praise. They crumple the copies of
the rant, tear them and tread on them.*

ABRAHAM MEN. With derry hey down doe
We cheer the crown and sceptre
This Queen who rules us now
We shall not look for better.

ELIZABETH. I die, I die, at last I die. Let me lie languorous in
state a full month upon a thick bed of ostrich plumes. Then
bear my body slowly down the lapping river on a black
draped barge towards my earthly grave. Send for my cousin
James. I have played my part.

She dies. The ABRAHAM MEN *pick her up and carry her off,
moving slowly, a funeral barge drifting down the river.* LUCIUS
and BEATRICE, *on opposite sides of the stage, watch. The singing
swells up.* ELIZABETH *is transformed into a legend.*

ABRAHAM MEN. With derry hey down doe
We cheer the crown and sceptre
This Queen who leaves us now
We never loved a better.

In sombre mood, they bear ELIZABETH *out of sight, singing the
stanza over and over again.*

LUCIUS *is sitting on the ground.* BEATRICE *looks at him for a
moment, then goes.* WARBURTON, *carrying a copy of the rant,
approaches* LUCIUS *slowly. Some moments, then* LUCIUS *looks up
and sees* WARBURTON. WARBURTON *waves the printed page
at* LUCIUS *and smiles.*

WARBURTON. One of yours?

LUCIUS *says nothing.*

Don't deny it. I recognise your style. You're an artist. You
leave fingerprints.

LUCIUS. Not as many as I used to.

WARBURTON. You shouldn't have taken what she did
personally.

LUCIUS. It wasn't that.

WARBURTON. You were lucky, just getting a hand chopped. She spoke very warmly of you, you know.

LUCIUS. It wasn't that, it was –

WARBURTON. Yes?

LUCIUS *rages.*

LUCIUS. I wanted . . . to do something. To make things move forward. Just in some small . . . To change something!

LUCIUS *makes a grab for* WARBURTON, *tries to hit him. Quickly, the* GUARD *appears from out of the shadows and holds* LUCIUS *from behind.*

GUARD. I told you before son, tread warily.

LUCIUS *struggles, but to no avail.*

LUCIUS. I . . . I . . . I . . .

WARBURTON. She was only a monarch. There'll be another one along in a minute.

LUCIUS (*quietly*). I wanted.

WARBURTON. You were funny. Why wasn't that enough?

LUCIUS. I wanted.

WARBURTON. I'm sorry. It'll be the Clink for you. Then Tyburn though there won't be any hurry. No one to sign the death warrants for a while. It's nothing personal. I always liked you.

WARBURTON *goes.*

GUARD. And I didn't. What's the odds? Come on, we're moving.

The GUARD *drags* LUCIUS *upstage. Melancholic violin.*

ZANDA *appears from the shadows.*

ZANDA. Cowl up. Face down. Walk. Staring at the ground. Walk away. Don't let your face be seen. Walk. All the way to Wales. Find a cave. Stay there. Eat grass and berries. Nothing happens. It gets warm. You lie outside the cave at night. Then it gets cooler. The cold. You watch the water dripping from the icicles on the roof of the cave. You wait for the winter to end. But it doesn't. The icicles grow longer. One day, like an animal, you decide the winter is over. It isn't, but your body tells you to go. So you stand up and walk. Walk back. Wondering what happened to the spring. Walking on ice, sleeping on ice. Back to London. After a year. Where the voices in the river are silenced. Where even the river is ice.

Around ZANDA, *the* ICE-DWELLERS *begin to take their places for the final scene.*

Scene Nineteen
THE ICE

One year later. The Thames is frozen over. It's early evening. A small society of ice-dwellers in tents has sprung up. A half-hearted market is going on. The people are the ABRAHAM MEN, *but they no longer think and move as a group. Everyone is in a separate, individual world. The mood is subdued. Some people are preparing to get off the river, perhaps anticipating a thaw. As the scene progresses, this becomes a general exodus.* BUTLER *is there, bartering with a* STALLHOLDER. *He seems to have aged more than a year. The only figure who does not move in the scene is* LUCIUS *who is sitting, manacled, with his legs in the stocks. The stocks are embedded in the ice.*

BEATRICE *comes on carrying a begging bowl. She sings and holds out the bowl to passers-by.*

BEATRICE. Throughout the reign of Lillybet
    The people all were jolly-o
    The Thames ran warm, the Thames ran wet
    And fools did play at folly-o.

    And now throughout the reign of James
    The people all are jollier
    For never cooler ran the Thames
    Nor ever fools were follier.

    BEATRICE *goes off singing.*

    BUTLER *goes over to speak to* LUCIUS.

BUTLER. Still around then.

LUCIUS. You could call it that.

BUTLER. While since I've seen you.

LUCIUS. The Clink.

BUTLER. Yeah? Me too. I done a year. They let me out three weeks ago. Keep me head down now. Best.

LUCIUS. Yeah?

WARBURTON *comes on. He watches the* ICE-DWELLERS *leaving.*

BUTLER. Can't say I go a bundle on James. Almost miss her in fact. You knew where you were.

LUCIUS. I suppose.

BUTLER *shows* LUCIUS *something.*

BUTLER. Got this old key in the market today. Might be useful.

LUCIUS. What for?

BUTLER. Something. I dunno. Funny weather we've been getting. They're talking about a thaw. I don't see it. I like the river frozen. Makes London bigger. Well, be seeing you.

LUCIUS. No, I don't think so.

BUTLER. Well then, so long. Keep your nose clean.

He shuffles off.

WARBURTON. I'm glad we've finally settled your case. The King was sentimental about executions at first. Worried he might be snuffing out his own supporters. But they learn. Good learners, monarchs.

LUCIUS. Have to be.

WARBURTON. There's a different approach in many ways. But I'm valued. Continuity from reign to reign. Contacts in Europe and so on.

LUCIUS. I never told you. Your plot. It was class. You've got a flair for all that stuff. Shame you got what you wanted.

BEATRICE *returns with her begging bowl, still singing.*

BEATRICE. Dost thou know the price of wheat
Oh my fair young lady
Canst thou say how I may eat
Oh my bonny lady?

Canst thou ever say for sure
When the raindrops next shall pour
When the wolf will reach your door

Lady, lady?

Canst thou know the price of corn
Oh my white-haired lady
Canst thou say why I was born
Oh my sainted lady?

She holds out the begging bowl to WARBURTON.

BEATRICE. Got any coin for me, sir? Groat, anything. Sir? Or make me a fine match. Anything?

WARBURTON *reaches in his purse. Gives her coins.*

Thank you sir. I had a silver pistol once, but that went. I can't say where.

BEATRICE *goes off singing softly.*

LUCIUS. Still. You've got your job, that's the main thing.
    WARBURTON *gives him a hard look.*

WARBURTON. I was just crossing the river. Thought I'd say goodbye.

LUCIUS. You save money on ferries this weather, I suppose.

WARBURTON. It helps. Enjoy the evening.

WARBURTON *goes.* ZANDA *walks towards* LUCIUS, *keeping her eye on* WARBURTON.

LUCIUS. What happened to you?

ZANDA. I went away.

LUCIUS. Why did you come back?

ZANDA. Settle my debts.

She pulls out the silver pistol from under her cloak. Shows LUCIUS. *Puts it back.*

LUCIUS. Make sure it doesn't happen in my line of vision. I think I'm in enough trouble.

ZANDA. I told you not to do your act.

ZANDA *goes, pursuing* WARBURTON.

LUCIUS. Yes, I had advice from higher up, I seem to remember.

The last of the ice-dwellers has drifted away. LUCIUS *sits in the stocks on his own. A pause. There is a shot.* LUCIUS *does not react.*

Some moments, then a huddled, cowled FIGURE *comes on carrying a sack from the opposite direction to the shot. It walks past* LUCIUS, *then stops, turns, stands. It is* THOMAS. LUCIUS *is staring ahead of him.* THOMAS'*s face is still hidden in his cowl.*

THOMAS. By the mass. If 'tis not Signor Bordello, newly come, or so his gait betells, from some house of drabbery.

LUCIUS *turns.* THOMAS *removes his cowl.*

LUCIUS. Thomas.

THOMAS. So. Did it go down well, the new comedy?

LUCIUS. They liked it, yes. They liked it a lot, only . . .

THOMAS. It annoyed someone.

LUCIUS. Yes. Yes, it did. Being funny . . . carries certain responsibilities.

THOMAS. I wouldn't know.

LUCIUS. What?

THOMAS. Three days without you. Doing the act. I realised I'm not funny. Why didn't you tell me?

LUCIUS. I was being polite.

THOMAS. Booed off in Dulwich. Canterbury they threw a joint of bacon at me.

LUCIUS. Not bad.

THOMAS. It was still alive. Dover, they didn't let me onstage, word had got round. Got a passage to France. Fell in with some musicians. Good crowd, picked it up. Come back to start my own band.

LUCIUS. Nice one.

Pause.

THOMAS. How can I get you out?

LUCIUS. It's . . . honestly, it's not going to be possible.

THOMAS. No?

LUCIUS. These people I've annoyed. Quite powerful.

THOMAS. How long will you be here?

LUCIUS. Till dawn.

THOMAS. Well that's not so bad.

LUCIUS. Think about it.

Pause.

THOMAS. If it stays cold. You'll die. Exposure. If it gets warmer, the ice will crack. You'll sink.

LUCIUS. That's it. Jacobean punishment. It's more intellectual than what we're used to.

THOMAS. I could –

LUCIUS. Bring me some gruel? No. The guards have got orders.

THOMAS. I could . . . There must be something.

LUCIUS. There's nothing.

THOMAS. There must be something, I'm your brother for Christ's sake.

LUCIUS. No you're not.

THOMAS. What?

LUCIUS. Didn't you know that? You were just a stray they took pity on.

THOMAS. I don't . . . you never told me.

LUCIUS. We don't look remotely alike, did you never notice that?

Pause.

THOMAS. No. Never thought.

LUCIUS. Take it or leave it.

THOMAS. You're still my brother.

LUCIUS. Thank you. But there's nothing you can do.

THOMAS. No. I'm sorry.

LUCIUS. What d'you think'll be better, freezing or drowning?

THOMAS. If it melts . . . there's a chance . . . you could float . . .

LUCIUS *rattles the heavy chains.*

Oh. Well. If you could find a way to keep warm.

LUCIUS. I could run up and down, yeah.

THOMAS. Sorry. Dawn is it?

LUCIUS. Dawn.

THOMAS. I'll come out, first light, whatever the weather. If it melts, I'll get a boat. I won't let you down. Bury you next to father.

LUCIUS. Nice thought.

THOMAS. Trust me.

THOMAS *goes over to* LUCIUS. *They embrace.*

THOMAS. Well.

THOMAS *starts to go. Then turns.*

Just an idea. Keep you warm for a bit. Try it, you're a natural.

THOMAS *drops his sack at the foot of the stocks. Goes.*

LUCIUS *looks at the sack. Reaches down, delves in it. Brings out a violin. He looks at it with curiosity. Puts it to his chin, holds the bow with his stump, scrapes some tentative notes. Blows on his fingers.*

LUCIUS. I'm a natural.

He plays. Suddenly he's brilliant, inspired. He sits in the stocks, playing a soaring violin solo, full of dread and passion, like a file scraping on the bars of a prison.

Blackout.

The End.